The Disinformers

MEDIA AND PUBLIC AFFAIRS

Robert Mann, Series Editor

The Disinformers

Social Media, Disinformation, and Elections

Edited by Lance Porter

LOUISIANA STATE UNIVERSITY PRESS BATON ROUGE

Published by Louisiana State University Press
lsupress.org

LSU Press Paperback Original

DESIGNER: Barbara Neely Bourgoyne
TYPEFACE: Calluna

Cataloging-in-Publication Data are available from the Library of Congress

ISBN 978-0-8071-8258-1 (pbk.: alk. paper) — ISBN 978-0-8071-8362-5 (pdf) —
ISBN 978-0-8071-8361-8 (epub)

CONTENTS

ACKNOWLEDGMENTS

I would like to acknowledge the work of some key contributors to this project, none of whom are credited authors but all of whom were central to this work. This project grew out the 2020 John Breaux Symposium. The Reilly Center for Media and Public Affairs hosts this event every spring in the Manship School of Mass Communication at Louisiana State University. Reilly Center director Dr. Jenée Slocum came up with the concept for the program and asked me if I would organize the academic portions of the event and if I would put together an edited volume authored by its participants. I was honored that Jenée would ask me and more than a little intimidated by the excellent work produced from previous years. LSU and Manship are lucky to have such a passionate leader in Jenée, who brings the best people in the world on important and timely topics every year.

Speaking of the people who came to LSU to speak on this topic, I want to thank my coauthors. While I've spent much of my career studying digital and social media and their effects, I have not done much work on the topic of disinformation, so I knew I would need some help. Luckily, I know some amazing scholars who work in this area, and I knew this would be a great excuse to invite them to LSU and to work on a fun project with them. I'm grateful for the authors' participation in this book and the larger group that participated in the symposium.

Reilly Center program coordinator Kelci Sibley was integral in bringing these great people to campus, planning the event, and keeping everyone rested, fed, and happy. She is a master at what she does. I am thankful for her professionalism and superior organizational skills, an area in which I always need help.

I was fortunate to work with Pam Labbe as my research assistant as she was wrapping up her PhD in the Manship School. Pam brought many years of editing experience to this project, and I am grateful for her excellent suggestions on making each essay flow better. Her edits helped this book immensely.

As the organizer of two previous Breaux symposia and the author of two resulting edited volumes, my close friend Josh Grimm served as an effective sounding board for my ideas and an excellent motivator when times were tough. He listened patiently to my ideas and nodded thoughtfully at my frustrations in trying to get this thing completed. It wasn't easy.

We gathered for this event on March 5, 2020, and I remember some panelists starting to avoid shaking hands as COVID was just making its presence known in our area of the world. Little did we know that our world would totally shut down less than a week after the event. Our timeline for publication was starting to shift.

Editor James Long at the LSU Press was incredibly patient with me as the project was delayed time and again, through a pandemic and the loss of our good friend and leader, Dean Martin Johnson. My administrative duties shifted in the wake of Martin's death, but James was unwavering in his support of the project though all these challenges. My coauthors also stuck with me through these delays, and I'm especially grateful for their patience.

Finally, I would like to thank my dear wife, Leslie, for her unconditional love and support during the writing of this book. I would not have finished this project if it wasn't for you.

The Disinformers

Introduction

· · ·

LANCE PORTER

In the months leading up to the U.S. presidential election, Donald Trump claimed the election was rigged. He made this claim on his social media platform of choice, Twitter.

"Of course, there is large scale voter fraud happening on or before election day. Why do Republican leaders deny what is going on? So naive!"

As his poll numbers slipped, he began to intensify those claims in interviews and at his rallies, urging his supporters to monitor polling places located in swing states. Mike Pence seemed to contradict Trump, appearing on NBC's *Meet the Press* to declare that they would "absolutely" accept the results of the election. However, Trump advisor Rudy Giuliani made the rounds on the same television shows to echo Trump's allegations, saying he would have to be a "moron" to think the elections were fair. Media pundits began to worry what all of this meant for an already divided country (Roth 2016; "U.S. Elections," 2016). Would Trump's supporters refuse to accept the results of the election? Would there be a loss of faith in American democracy or even violence? However, there was one problem. Trump actually won this election. The year was 2016, not 2020.

The roots of the Big Lie of 2020 and the resulting January 6 insurrection run deep. In fact, Trump's claims embrace a long-running disinformation campaign. Trump has made election-fraud claims for many years, even before he entered the political arena. When President Barack Obama won reelection in 2012, Trump claimed the election was a "total sham," taking to Twitter to say, "We can't let this happen. We should march on Washington and stop this travesty. Our nation is totally divided!" (Smith 2020). When he began his campaign for president in 2016, he again used social media to take aim at his primary opponent, Ted Cruz, after losing the Iowa Caucus in February of 2016. He tweeted: "Ted Cruz didn't win Iowa, he stole it. That is why all of the polls were so wrong and why he got far more votes than anticipated. Bad!" and later, "Based on the fraud committed by Senator Ted Cruz during the Iowa Caucus, either a new election should take place or Cruz results nullified." A few weeks later, in February of 2016, longtime Trump advisor and self-proclaimed dirty trickster, Roger Stone, registered the URL "StoptheSteal.org" (Kuznia et al. 2020). Despite having lost the 2020 election and having incited a violent insurrection, Trump continues to make those bogus claims today. The results are profound. During Biden's presidency, polling has consistently shown that only one-fifth to one-quarter of Republicans believe that Biden won the 2020 election (Homans 2022).

Given Trump's unprecedented fraud claims in the lead-up to the 2016 election, independent nonprofit investigative news organization ProPublica decided to act, forming the largest-ever collaboration among journalists around a single event (Klein 2017). Over eleven hundred journalists and technologists from ProPublica, Google News Lab, USA Today, and Univision, along with journalism students from a dozen universities across the country, partnered to monitor not the election results, but the election process. The late Steve Buttry was head of Louisiana State University student media at the time, and he asked if we could partner and set up in the lab I direct, the Social Media Analysis and Creation (SMAC) Lab on election day. We recruited about a dozen students and spent hours training them to monitor social media posts and Google searches related to voting on election day. We anxiously set up at 5 a.m. on November 8, 2016, and fired up multiple monitors in the lab. Students rotated each hour to different monitoring stations. We held hourly teleconferences with the central newsroom in New York to make sure everyone was aware of what was going on across the nation. Gannett reporters on the ground in all fifty states investigated social media posts of any sort of voting-machine irregularities, long lines, or voter intimidation. As the hours ticked by, our excitement began to wane. As we shut things down at 10 p.m., I realized how sound our election systems actually were. We had not fielded a single legitimate complaint in our region. Across the nation, there were approximately half a dozen legitimate concerns raised. I came away from the project bored but buoyed by the soundness of our election systems.

Therefore, I was shocked that Trump's allegations of fraud led to the events of January 6, 2021. How could we have ended up here? With the rise of the commercial World Wide Web in the mid-1990s, the promise by many techno-utopians was that, with the Internet, everyone could be a publisher. Therefore, our information-communication systems would be democratized. All you needed was an easily affordable Internet connection, and you could publish the information of your choice, and it would live on equal footing with the *New York Times.* No longer would we be forced to choose among three broadcast networks and print publications produced by moneyed publishers. We would have literally millions of channels to choose from. We could even start our own channels! Unfortunately, the fact that anyone could be a publisher also ushered in the idea that bad actors could publish alongside the *New York Times.* Disinformation has a rich history in American politics, with the term *disinformation* dating back to the 1950s (Manning et al. 2004), and the Russian government has long attempted to sow disinformation in western democracies, but somehow the 2016 election was different.

The 2016 presidential election saw a "sweeping and systematic" (Walton 2019, 107) attack intended to influence the results in favor of Donald Trump, and that election also marked the first time that fringe right-wing conspiracy theories of the birther movement and the John

Birch Society were part of a major party's nominee's political strategy (Homans 2022). While Trump's claims of fraud in the 2016 and 2020 elections were not accurate, disinformation had undoubtedly wreaked havoc on our media system. We still need to understand what happened. Therefore, this collection of essays and research will take a look at this turning point of 2016 and even a bit beyond as some of the work featured here follows 2016 disinformation campaigns over into the 2018 U.S. midterm elections.

The diverse ideas collected here are from a cross section of researchers working across the fields of communication, mass communication, political science, and computer science. Researchers offer essays, data analysis, and even something that academics are not always comfortable discussing: potential solutions to our disinformation problem.

We start with Russia. In the first essay, Josephine Lukito sets the stage by taking a close look at a well-known state-sponsored disinformation campaign by examining the Russian Internet Research Agency's (IRA) multiyear campaign to influence the 2016 U.S. presidential election. Her work is prescient in that it takes a larger look at the implications of these types of campaigns and their broader impact on public trust in our political system. Her work provides baseline definitions of the terms we will be using throughout this work, such as *disinformation, misinformation,* and *propaganda.*

What were the platforms doing to combat this operation? Shouldn't the U.S. government step in to defend our media systems? In the second essay, David Karpf provides an educated perspective on the role digital platforms play in the proliferation of misinformation and disinformation and what the U.S. government should do about their role. He makes a powerful argument for why these platforms need to be regulated, but he strikes a realistic note on the challenges our government will face in the current regulatory environment.

While trolls and malicious political actors are certainly behind much of the spread of political disinformation on social media, it's ordinary people who are most responsible for sharing political disinformation (Dupuis and Williams 2019). We know that those who get most of their news from social media are less knowledgeable and less engaged than those who get their news from other sources (Pew Research Center 2020). We also know that this same group of people who do not pay much attention to the news are the least concerned about the effects of disinformation on the election (Pew Research Center 2019). In the third essay, Itai Himelboim, Dror Walter, and Yotam Ophir examine the Twitter bios of the users who both introduce and spread misinformation—information that is demonstrably not true, but that the users may believe is true. Using machine learning to create thematic personae, Himelboim and his colleagues identify important differences between content introducers and content spreaders, providing a new method to categorize and identify those responsible for misinformation.

Similarly, we know that critical comments from other users work better than disclaimers posted by social media companies to dissuade people from sharing disinformation (Colliander 2019). However, what happens when there is a void of critical information within a community? What if that community is historically marginalized? In the fourth essay, Claudia Flores-Saviaga and Saiph Savage use two large-scale data sets taken from The_Donald, one of the most notorious communities on Reddit, to analyze how political trolls used conventional social media community-building strategies to spread hateful content and disinformation in the Latinx community during the 2016 U.S. presidential election and the 2018 midterm elections. Their findings show how trolls used disinformation, harassment, propaganda, and even gamification to disenfranchise Latinx voters, ultimately causing some to pull away from online conversations and platforms.

How does technology enable disinformation? In the fifth essay, Golden G. Richard III provides a cybersecurity perspective on disinformation. He illustrates how sophisticated communication technologies are in place that will cause disinformation problems to worsen in the coming years. Modern malware is capable of not only targeting citizens, but also making them unwilling accomplices in disinformation. After detailing these risks, Richard provides some technical and structural methods to investigate and combat disinformation.

Is the disinformation from the Big Lie endemic to American elections, or do other countries face similar challenges? In the sixth essay, Jacob Groshek and Sander Andreas Schwartz provide an international perspective by comparatively modeling the 2018 U.S. midterm elections and the 2019 Danish general elections on social media. The authors use social network analysis to identify important differences between the two election systems, pointing out the proliferation of bots in the United States and the greater participation by politicians in Denmark. However, they ultimately make a strong case for more journalists to step up and participate in social media conversations.

Where do we go from here? In the last essay, Jakob Ohme provides a glimpse of the future of disinformation effects by examining the first generation of citizens to come of age as digital natives. How will growing up amid a media environment where disinformation proliferates affect democratic actions? Will young voters think it normal that people decide what is true by searching for information that supports their own beliefs, or will they become hypercritical sophisticated consumers of information? Ohme approaches these questions using empirical data on voter mobilization, ultimately providing a way forward for society to help young citizens navigate a media world filled with increasing levels of disinformation.

REFERENCES

Colliander, J. 2019. "'This Is Fake News': Investigating the Role of Conformity to Other Users' Views When Commenting on and Spreading Disinformation in Social Media." *Computers in Human Behavior* 97: 20215. www.sciencedirect.com/science/article/abs/pii/S074756321930130X.

Dupuis, M. J., and A. Williams. 2019. "The Spread of Disinformation on the Web: An Examination of Memes on Social Networking." IEEE SmartWorld, Ubiquitous Intelligence and Computing, Advanced and Trusted Computing, Scalable Computing and Communications, Cloud and Big Data Computing, Internet of People, and Smart City Innovation (SmartWorld/SCALCOM/UIC/ATC/CBDCom/IOP/SCI). Leicester, UK, 1412–18. doi.10.1109/SmartWorld-UIC-ATC-SCALCOM-IOP-SCI.2019.00256.

Homans, C. 2022. "How 'Stop the Steal' Captured the American Right." July 19. *New York Times.* www.nytimes.com/2022/07/19/magazine/stop-the-steal.html.

Klein, S. 2017. *Electionland: The Inside Story.* May 4. ProPublica. www.propublica.org/article/electionland-the-inside-story.

Kuznia, R., R. K. Griffin, N. Curt Devine, and D. Black. 2020. "Stop the Steal's Massive Disinformation Campaign Connected to Roger Stone." CNN. www.cnn.com/2020/11/13/business/stop-the-steal-disinformation-campaign-invs/index.html.

Manning, M. J., M. Manning, and H. Romerstein. 2004. *Historical Dictionary of American Propaganda.* Westport, CT: Greenwood Publishing Group.

Pew Research Center. 2019. "Growing and Improving Pew Research Center's American Trends Panel." February.

———. 2020. "Americans Who Mainly Get Their News on Social Media Are Less Engaged, Less Knowledgeable." July.

Roth, Z. 2016. "Donald Trump's 'Rigged Election' Claims Raise Historical Alarms." October 17. *NBC News.* www.nbcnews.com/politics/2016-election/donald-trump-s-rigged-election-claims-raise-historical-alarms-n667831.

Smith, T. 2020. "Trump Has Longstanding History of Calling Elections 'Rigged' If He Doesn't Like the Results." November 11. ABC News. abcnews.go.com/Politics/trump-longstanding-history-calling-elections-rigged-doesnt-results/story?id=74126926.

"US Election 2016: Trump Says Election 'Rigged at Polling Places.'" October 17. *BBC News.* www.bbc.com/news/election-us-2016-37673797.

Walton, C. 2019. "Spies, Election Meddling, and Disinformation: Past and Present." *Brown Journal of World Affairs* 26(1): 107–24.

Understanding a Case of State-Sponsored Digital Disinformation

Russia's Internet Research Agency

• • •

JOSEPHINE LUKITO

In August 2017, local Cleveland shock jock and "sports troll" Chris Mc-Neil posted a photo of a crowd, claiming that it was a rally for President Trump in Phoenix. It was shared widely on Twitter, due in part to the conservative-leaning handle @TEN_GOP, whose tweet with the image (unattributed to McNeil) received thousands of likes and retweets. Several hours later, @TEN_GOP took the image down once it was revealed that the photo was of a Cleveland Cavaliers parade and not a Trump rally. Liberal-leaning news organizations pounced on the opportunity to mock conservatives for distributing false information, often using screenshots of @TEN_GOP's tweets as evidence of "incompetency" (for example, Collins 2017).

But as it turns out, the falsely attributed image was not the only lie. Two months later, Twitter announced it had suspended @TEN_GOP, along with thousands of other human-controlled and bot-run accounts managed by the Internet Research Agency, Russia's troll army and a known disseminator of political disinformation. At the time of its suspension, @TEN_GOP had over 100,000 followers (Rizoiu et al. 2018). At no point did it appear that anyone—including prominent Republicans,

Democrats, and news media who interacted with the handle—realized the account was controlled by a Russian operative.

This anecdote illustrates some of the ways state-sponsored disinformation actors exploit and poison the political communication system to spread disinformation. In this essay I discuss how and why countries use digital disinformation to manipulate political discourse in foreign countries. To explore this phenomenon, I focus on Russia's Internet Research Agency (IRA), which maintained a multiyear disinformation campaign targeting the United States during and after the 2016 U.S. presidential election. This is one of the best-known instances of a state-sponsored digital disinformation campaign. The Internet Research Agency's tactics have inspired other countries to deploy their own disinformation campaigns (Martin, Shapiro, and Nedashkovskaya 2019). Though there is significant disagreement as to whether these disinformation campaigns do in fact "influence" elections and votes in favor of the disinformation producer, state-sponsored disinformation has distressing implications beyond the voting booth, especially including the degradation of people's trust in political discourse. These longer-term issues compound already existing contention within the public sphere, potentially exacerbating polarization and discouraging political engagement.

Definitions

Because disinformation scholarship draws from multiple disciplines, including national security, international communication, and political communication research, I begin with several definitions. First *disinformation* refers to messages that intentionally contain false or misleading features. Though we typically understand disinformation as false or doctored information, messages from false personae or messages that are artificially made to look popular are also forms of disinformation. Disinformation is different from, but related to, other types of messages in the information disorder, including *misinformation,* when someone does not realize what they are sharing is false; *mal-information,* when verifiably accurate information is spread to serve a malicious intent

(Wardle 2018; Freelon and Wells 2020); and bullshit, which includes statements made "without any real regard for truth or falsity" (Blevins et al. 2021; Frankfurt 2005). A *disinformation campaign* refers to the strategic production of disinformation over a period of time to serve a malicious, often political, goal (Lukito 2020). Unlike individual disinformation messages, campaigns are (1) strategic (that is, goal-oriented) and (2) systematic, involving the continual production of multiple messages for some period of time.

Though many individuals and groups produce disinformation, this essay focuses on state-sponsored disinformation in social media content. State-sponsored disinformation is a form of *propaganda*—messages that are meant to influence the opinions or perceptions of an audience (Gelders and Ihlen 2010). While the definition is relatively innocuous, propaganda is generally considered a pejorative term, related to manipulative and deceptive intent (Huckin 2016). Propaganda strategies can be typologized on a continuum (Gray and Martin 2007). On one side of the spectrum is *white propaganda,* in which the country explicitly states its affiliation in a message (public diplomacy is often considered a modern form of white propaganda) (Melissen 2011). On the other end is *black propaganda,* when the country obscures its role in the message production. State-sponsored disinformation campaigns are a form of black propaganda (Garner 2010).

As people began to use the Internet to engage in political discourse, states adapted disinformation strategies to digital platforms, particularly social media networks like Twitter and WhatsApp. This form of disinformation is called *computational propaganda;* it involves the manipulation of advantages specific to digital communication, including automation and the tracking of audience metrics (Woolley and Howard 2018).

Several national security terms are also worth noting. *Propaganda* is often used interchangeably with the concept of *psychological warfare,* referring to strategies employed by countries to evoke a psychological reaction from people (Speier 1948). Digital disinformation campaigns fall into the purview of *cyberwarfare,* which includes tactics such as cyber-espionage and hacking (Shah 2011). The combination of cyberwarfare and psychological warfare is sometimes called *cyber propaganda* (Al-Khateeb, Hussain, and Agarwal 2019).

Why Focus on State-Sponsored Disinformation?

Historically, state-sponsored disinformation can be found across time in various forms. Both democratic and autocratic countries have used disinformation, particularly throughout the Cold War (for U.S. disinformation in Latin America, see Ferreira 2008; for Soviet disinformation, see Romerstein 2001) or during other wartimes (for example, de Lame 2005). These state governments systematized the production of disinformation and incorporated disinformation tactics into broader psychological warfare campaigns (Bittman 1981).

State-sponsored disinformation campaigns targeting foreign audiences are worth special consideration given the international norms of "Westphalian sovereignty"—the principle that countries should not interject in the domestic affairs of other countries (Krasner 2001). This is especially relevant given that states often target foreign audiences for disinformation during elections and voting periods, an inherent violation of a country's sovereignty. Historically, this has not stopped modern nation-states from disseminating black propaganda to foreign audiences (for example, Doherty 1994). Democratic institutions are said to be particularly vulnerable to foreign disinformation, particularly during voting periods (Bennett and Livingston 2018). For example, during an election, a foreign government may try to persuade citizens to vote for a politician who is "friendly" to that foreign government. However, it is worth emphasizing that democratic nations themselves, including the United States, produce disinformation (Bittman 1990).

State governments are incentivized to use disinformation campaigns because they are substantially cheaper than military action or other diplomatic strategic (Abang and Okon 2018). Additionally, disinformation campaigns have been found to be more effective than other forms of propaganda that do not rely on deception (Martin 1982). Without international norms discouraging use of such campaigns, there is no reason why a country would not maintain a troll army.

State-Sponsored Disinformation
on Social Media

Digital media afford state governments an opportunity to influence public discourse directly and anonymously in a way that has never existed with other media technology. While digital media are accessible to all political actors (even an individual can become a political troll with relative ease), states have the capacity to utilize surveillance techniques and produce disinformation en masse, targeting foreign and domestic audiences to pursue their political goals. The digital affordances that allow anyone to be a message producer can be easily abused by those with traditional power, including and especially state governments (Pearce 2015).

Though states deploy disinformation on various digital platforms, social media networks have emerged as an effective medium for disinformation production and dissemination. In addition to having few gatekeepers, social media facilitates the production of short messages, which are easier to produce in large quantities, compared to long blog posts or artificial news articles. Through social media platforms, disinformation actors can communicate with opinion leaders like celebrities or politicians (Linvill and Warren 2020), target niche audiences with extreme controversial political viewpoints or unique issues (Xia et al. 2019), or even have their messages amplified beyond the social media platform, such as on news media (Lukito et al. 2020).

Three key aspects of digital communication benefit state-sponsored disinformation production: anonymity, audience metrics, and automated promotion. Anonymity is a controversial attribute of digital media as it simultaneously affords users privacy and allows malicious actors to easily conceal their identity. Because black propaganda relies on the ability to hide one's identity, the Internet is a prime space for state actors to spread disinformation. Disinformation producers may attempt to further obscure their true identity by using virtual private networks (VPNs) to conceal their IP addresses or to give the appearance that their IP address originates from somewhere else.

Digital technology provides unique opportunities to track a message's popularity as well. Audience metrics have become important measures that celebrities, public figures, advertisers, journalists, and disinformation actors closely watch (Baym 2013; Tandoc and Thomas 2014). Given that these metrics—including liking, sharing, commenting, and follower metrics—are readily available to any digital communicator, it behooves state-sponsored digital disinformation actors to study and learn from audience metrics.

Relatedly, actors are motivated to use automated or artificial means to make their messages or accounts appear more popular than they are (Santini et al. 2020). One common strategy is to use automated accounts, also known as "bots" (Woolley and Howard 2018). Bot accounts can "follow" other disinformation accounts managed by real people, making the latter appear more popular. Disinformation actors can use bots to share (or "retweet") and like disinformation content, increasing the messages' perceived social value. Another strategy that disinformation actors can use to manipulate their follower account is to buy followers from a third party (Dawson and Innes 2019).

Though any disinformation actor can (and do) exploit these considerations, state-sponsored production benefits from an overabundance of resources that allow it to scale up the production of digital disinformation. One person can produce only so much digital disinformation, but a government can hire hundreds of individuals to work together to conduct a digital disinformation campaign, using state-surveillance strategies to inform their content production. It is also worth reemphasizing that state-sponsored disinformation campaigns serve broader political goals, including framing discourse around national security affairs (for example, Gallacher et al. 2018), coordinating with other information warfare tactics like cyberattacks and hacks (Loui and Hope 2017), or damaging social media platforms as spaces for public discourse. For example, state-sponsored disinformation campaigns can help disseminate information that is stolen through other cyberwarfare strategies.

As of 2019, over forty-four government agencies employed some sort of social media disinformation campaign (Bradshaw and Howard 2019). One popular strategy is the use of social media troll armies, sometimes known as *troll farms*. Troll armies engage in the coordinated production of disinformation messages by humans using social media accounts with false identities. (These social media accounts are called *sock puppets*.)

The disinformation that troll armies produce is a form of *astroturfing* (Keller et al. 2020), a type of disinformation where messages funded by a government are meant to look like they come from regular people or grassroots organizers. In terms of content, state-sponsored troll armies produce and spread a variety of messages, including real and inflammatory information, false information, and false opinions. Because countries utilize troll armies to serve different purposes—including trying to make their own country look good, delegitimizing social movements, or framing public conversation about wedge issues—the disinformation messages are as varied as the goals they serve.

Relationships between governments and their troll armies vary greatly. Some countries simply outsource the production of disinformation to a private company (like the Operation Earnest Voice in the United States, which is maintained by the private company Ntrepid; see Imamverdiyev 2016). Alternatively, political operatives can play a more active role in the development of messages (like the 50 Cent Party, which is managed by Chinese authorities; see Yang, Yang and Wilson 2015). And yet others are somewhere in the middle, functioning as a somewhat independent group but with affiliations to government politicians (like Russia's Internet Research Agency).

Russian Disinformation

The Internet Research Agency is but one organization in a long history of disinformation use by Russia. Next, we explore the history of Russian disinformation that informed the development and effectiveness of the IRA.

Active Measures

Over the past century, the USSR/Russia has been among the most pro-
lific states in terms of disinformation production. The Soviet Union
began using disinformation since its inception, first through the KGB's
black propaganda department and later through the formalized "Directorate D" department (Romerstein 2001). By the 1960s, foreign-targeted
disinformation production was part of the USSR's *active measures* tactics:
a collection of strategies that targeted foreign countries and sought to
influence world events in the Soviet Union's favor (Abrams 2016). Active
measures are considered a form of psychological warfare (Sinclair 2016).

The goal of active measures–style disinformation is to mislead foreign audiences about political or social issues, to increase doubt about
the veracity of information in political discourse, and to sow discord
between different factions within a country's citizenry (Abrams 2016).
This is different from disinformation campaigns that are intended to
improve a country's brand, such as the United States' Operation Earnest Voice (Holtmann 2013). Publics and audiences, not political leaders
of foreign countries, are typically the direct targets of active measures
(Godson and Schultz 1985).

A key aspect of early Russian active measures was the exploitation
of political and social issues that stoked fear and distrust. For example,
during the Vietnam War, Soviet disinformation focused on chemical
warfare, a salient issue among the U.S. population at the time (Boghardt
2009). Another KGB disinformation campaign, Operation DENVER
(sometimes erroneously codenamed INFEKTION), promoted the idea
that the United States created HIV/AIDS as a biological weapon (Selvage
2019). These strategies exploited wedge issues of their time just as digital
disinformation campaigns focus on controversial issues today.

Russian active-measures strategies blended accurate and inaccurate
information. For example, Russian information-warfare strategies combined disinformation propaganda and *kompromat,* malicious true information about an opponent that is strategically leaked (Oates 2017; *kompromat* is comparable to mal-information in the information disorder;

see Wardle 2018). To further cast doubt on the accuracy of information in the political discourse, the Soviet Union / Russia exploited the role of news organization in disseminating information across the public sphere (Romerstein 2001). For example, the Internet Research Agency created accounts that impersonated news organizations (Kim et al. 2019), coordinated with state-sponsored, white propaganda news organizations (Zannettou et al. 2019), and manipulated unsuspecting, legitimate news organizations to spread disinformation (Lukito et al. 2020).

Because active measures are taken up by a state government, surveillance and disinformation production go hand in hand (Michaelsen and Galsius 2018). Surveillance contributes significantly to the effectiveness of a disinformation campaign, as understanding the political discursive terrain allows for the production of more salient, attention-getting, and persuasive disinformation. Relative to other actors, state governments have more resources to surveil both domestic and foreign publics (Krueger 2005).

Russian Digital Disinformation

Russia's long-term experimentation with active measures helped them adapt disinformation strategies that exploited digital media platforms. Digital communication presented Russia with an opportunity to expand and further develop their disinformation strategies both domestically and abroad. As a result, Russia's digital disinformation strategies are on the cutting edge.

Russia's foray into the digital disinformation arena began domestically. In its early years, the Internet was a new opportunity for Russian citizens to exchange and gain political information without the extreme, monopolistic government control over media production that typified the Russian media ecology. Unlike other countries, like China, Russia did not impose strong restrictions on digital political discourse; rather, Russians themselves set a high bar for the quality of information produced online, particularly in blogs (Sanovich 2017).

It is in this communication environment that Russian politicians, particularly Dmitry Medvedev, began to utilize digital media as platforms for propaganda dissemination. Targeting platforms such as LiveJournal, Facebook, and Yandex in 2011 (all popular social media platforms in Russia at the time), Medvedev began sharing information directly to his fans and followers within a year of entering office (Sanovich 2017). During that time, Medvedev employed ad hoc troll farms (also known as "web brigades"), born out of pro-Kremlin youth groups, to promote his blog posts. These nascent troll farms were responsible for amplifying Medvedev's messages, producing pro-Kremlin messages with extensive "proof" of different issues, and manipulating search-engine results to ensure pro-Kremlin accounts were listed at the top of social media results.

Not long after, these web brigades began targeting foreign audiences, first within Russia's geographic sphere of influence and then beyond. Foreign-targeted disinformation activities would be eventually coordinated through the Internet Research Agency, Russia's best-known state-sponsored troll army.

Russia's Internet Research Agency

The Internet Research Agency (IRA) is a disinformation production organization based in St. Petersburg that focuses on digital and social media campaigns. Founded in 2013 by Yevgeny Prigozhin (an ally of Russian president Vladimir Putin), the IRA was led by Mikhail Ivanovich Bystrov; Special Counsel Robert Mueller indicted Bystrov in 2018 (*United States of America [U.S.] v. Internet Research Agency LLC [IRA LLC]* 2018). As of 2014, the IRA employed over six hundred people (Seddon 2014), of whom ninety were specifically focused on the U.S. disinformation campaign, also known as the translation project (de Haldevang 2017).

The primary producers of disinformation are employees called "specialists." Specialists are put on specific teams that target different countries for disinformation and are paid around seven hundred dollars a month (Harris 2017). They work in eight- or twelve-hour shifts and have a quota of disinformation messages to produce during each shift. Specialists were pressured a great deal to achieve their message-production quota (Dawson and Innes 2019). According to interviews with former IRA employees, specialists receive an email at the beginning of their shift with directions about where to post and what kinds of messages to post. One former troll said, "They told you which topics you should comment on and how to write your comments. You just had to play with the words" (Marat Mindiyarov, quoted in Green 2018).

Specialists also receive regular feedback to improve the spread of disinformation; this feedback was informed by audience metrics and metadata about the popularity of certain social media messages (*U.S. v. IRA LLC* 2018). The IRA's process of producing disinformation has been described as "industrial" (Linvill and Warren 2020), which speaks to the sheer quantity of disinformation messages disseminated. In addition to specialists and data analysts, other departments were responsible for producing different types of content, like memes (Dawson and Innes 2019), perhaps suggesting an "assembly-line" style of disinformation production.

Within its first year, the Internet Research Agency began developing campaigns and disinformation teams that targeted foreign audiences outside of Russia. Early campaigns first targeted countries within their sphere of influence, including former USSR states and geographically proximate countries such as Ukraine (Mejias and Vokuev 2015). Because of Russia's geopolitical interests in the affairs of nearby countries, the relationship between the IRA's actions and Russia's known interests was much more obvious. For example, content produced by IRA specialists during the Euromaidan revolution in Ukraine focused primarily on anti-Ukraine rhetoric, the conflict in Donbass, and the annexation of Crimea, likely because of Russia's direct involvement (Doroshenko and Lukito 2019).

Though automation was an important aspect throughout all the Internet Research Agency's campaigns, the IRA had a variety of strategies for artificially gaining followers. For example, Ukrainian-targeted IRA Twitter accounts were more likely to purchase their followers, while U.S.-targeted IRA accounts were more likely to use follower fishing strategies, such as following hundreds of new accounts, waiting for them to "follow back," and then unfollowing them several days later (Dawson and Innes 2019). A third common strategy utilized in both campaigns was the internal maintenance of bots that followed human-controlled disinformation accounts and retweeted their messages (Badawy, Ferrara and Lerman 2018).

Even in these early campaigns, the Internet Research Agency impersonated regular people and produced propaganda masquerading as news content. Obscuring one's true identity (anonymity) and artificially performing another identity (astroturfing) persuasively was essential to these messages' success or popularity. One notable example of this is @riafanru, an IRA Twitter account that claimed to be a federal news agency. The accompanying riafan website went so far as to imitate the appearance of RIA news, a reputable news organization. In 2018 (three months after the IRA was indicted by the U.S. Department of Justice), the riafan website announced a new "information agency" called USA Really (Orr 2018).

Message optimization is another attribute of Russian disinformation, due in no small part to Russia's history with domestic search optimization manipulation (Sanovich 2017, 9). Modern Russian disinformation campaigns, for example, track the spread of disinformation messages in real time using audience metrics and metadata such as likes, retweets, and shares. By collecting this information Russian operatives were able to produce their messages for specific, niche audiences. Targeted disinformation was made all the easier to produce given digital affordances, like the ability to serve specific advertisements to target demographics (Etudo, Yoon, and Yaraghi 2019).

By 2014, the Internet Research Agency had expanded its disinformation campaigns to attack a variety of western countries, including the United Kingdom (Llewellyn et al. 2018) and the United States.

The Internet Research Agency's campaign targeting the United States around the time of the 2016 U.S. Presidential election is among the IRA's best-known campaigns because of its perceived effectiveness, and how long the campaign lasted, and the likelihood that a Russian disinformation campaign was still active during the election. The campaign, known as the "translator project," began in 2015. It targeted several popular U.S. social media platforms, including Facebook, Twitter, Tumblr, and Reddit. Some of these strategies appear to have been coordinated; for example, partisan IRA messages posted on Twitter may have been tested initially on Reddit (Lukito 2020). The Internet Research Agency also created complex online personae of individuals or groups with multiple online accounts, including email addresses, blogs, and social media accounts (for a case study of one such account, Jenna Abrams, see Xia et al. 2019).

Prior to the development of the translator project, Russian operatives visited the United States to gain more information about U.S. political discourse (Mueller 2019). This highlights a hybridity to Russia's digital disinformation campaigns: while disinformation actors produced false information on digital platforms, their strategies were shaped by traditional tactics, including in-person surveillance and the targeting of news media. By collecting this information, Russian operatives could optimize their messages to make them more effective. For example, Facebook advertisements purchased by the IRA were targeted to specific demographics and geographies (Etudo, Yoon, and Yaraghi 2019).

From mid-2015 to 2017, Internet Research Agency specialists produced an unprecedented amount of online political disinformation in English, not only on the 2016 presidential election but on a range of salient political issues. During that time, the IRA produced or retweeted 1,886,919 Twitter messages, commented on or produced 12,603 Reddit posts, and purchased 3,126 Facebook advertisements, costing slightly over $100,000 (Lukito 2020; Spangher et al. 2020). The quantity of messages produced would have been difficult to achieve for one individual, or even a group, highlighting a key advantage of government-backed disinformation campaigns.

While not all the messages were political in nature, a substantial amount focused on political or social issues. As Xia et al. (2019) note, the combination of political and nonpolitical content helped IRA accounts create authentically perceived personae. (Nonpolitical content included tweeting inspirational quotes and playing hashtag games.) Based on the Mueller report (2019), the short-term goals of the campaign included supporting then-candidates Donald Trump and Sen. Bernie Sanders. However, the long-term goals of the IRA focused on sowing discord into U.S. social media discourse about politics (Mueller 2019)—this is in line with traditional active measure goals.

In their political content, IRA disinformation agents focused on salient and controversial wedge issues, including sanctuary cities, LGBTQ+ rights, Syria, and police brutality. Linvill and Warren (2020) typologized U.S.-targeting IRA Twitter handles into five categories: "right troll, left troll, news feed, hashtag games, and fearmonger" (5). Researchers have found that a large amount of IRA social media accounts impersonated individuals and groups from two politically active movements: the far right and Black Lives Matter. Conservative accounts seem to constitute a plurality of the Twitter accounts produced by the IRA (Bastos and Farkas 2019), and these accounts took advantage of the dense conservative social media network to disseminate salient, incendiary content (for more on the conservative network, see Blevins et al. 2021). But, in their study of how Russian disinformation actors engaged in digital blackfacing, Freelon et al. (2020) found that impersonating a Black activist produced the greatest amount of engagement for Russian IRA content. On Facebook, IRA accounts impersonating Black activists created and promoted false rallies and protests. (IRA accounts also promoted social movement events created by others.) One possible reason for impersonating these groups is to exploit their large and well-developed networks (Crosset, Tanner, and Campana 2019).

These disinformation-trolling efforts were supplemented with additional tactics, including using bots to amplify specialist-written messages (Woolley and Howard 2018); purchasing advertisements, particularly on Facebook (Etudo, Yoon, and Yaraghi 2019); and financially supporting a hundred U.S. activists, who did not realize they were being bankrolled in part by a Russian organization (de Haldevang 2017).

Effects of Russian Disinformation in the 2016 U.S. Presidential Election

Substantial disagreement exists regarding the effectiveness of Russian disinformation. Typically, scholars evaluate the Internet Research Agency's effectiveness based on whether the disinformation content persuaded citizens to vote for Donald Trump. Simply put, if the IRA helped President Trump get elected, then the disinformation campaign was successful. This is the argument put forth by Ruck et al. (2019), who showed that IRA Twitter activity could predict U.S. election polls. (This relationship may be bidirectional; see Lukito 2020.) Rather than focusing on the whole time span, Jamieson (2018) concentrates specifically on how Russian disinformation actors helped sway opinions a month before the campaign, particularly once the Podesta emails were leaked.

However, there are as many scholars who argue that Russian disinformation did not help President Trump get elected and was therefore ineffective. This research emphasizes the already polarized nature of U.S. political discourse. In other words, the IRA was not doing anything that domestic political operatives were not already doing themselves (Bail et al. 2020). Researchers making this argument also distinguish between exposure and persuasion: just because a person saw an IRA message does not necessarily mean they were persuaded by it. Ultimately, this body of literature argues that Russian disinformation was ineffective because it is improbable that simply being exposed to one IRA message would produce enough of a media effect as to sway a person's vote.

Regardless of the conclusion, our conceptualization of "effectiveness" has been quite narrow, focusing specifically on the 2016 election and on voting behavior in particular. However, this perspective ignores the many ways in which IRA operatives influenced U.S. political discourse, including exploiting activists, politicians, and even news media to amplify and disseminate their messages as misinformation. For example, many news outlets unintentionally embedded IRA tweets in at least one news story, often as an exemplar of American opinions (Lukito et al. 2020). These tactics helped IRA accounts grow their audience. Zhang et al. (under review) found that being quoted in partisan-aligned news media or interacting with partisan-aligned Twitter accounts helped grow the followings of IRA accounts; in other words, when conservative media quoted conservative IRA accounts, these accounts gained more followers the next day.

Because Russian disinformation strategies have traditionally exploited news organizations, the U.S. news-media ecosystem was especially vulnerable to disinformation actors who wanted to target and exploit the position of the press in the public sphere. For example, several IRA Twitter accounts pretended to be news organizations, using handles such as @TodayPittsburgh and @TodayBostonMA (House Intelligence Committee 2017). Accounts often mentioned news organizations like CNN, hoping to receive some attention. Though Russia's state-sponsored news organizations are older than the Internet Research Agency (RT, formerly Russia Today, was launched in 2005), the promotion of RT content in IRA social media messages (Zannettou et al. 2019) and the embedding of IRA tweets in RT content (Lukito et al. 2020) reveals how countries can coordinate white and black propaganda strategies across multiple media platforms. However, these considerations are not taken into account with a narrow focus on IRA disinformation and voting.

To really understand the impact of Russian disinformation on U.S. democratic institutions, it is necessary to expand our consideration of what constitutes "effective" disinformation, going beyond voting to account for the toxic impact of disinformation in public spheres. If political discourses are essential to healthy democracies (McLaverty 2002), then disinformation campaigns should be considered specially designed weapons that states use to target public spheres, exploit authentic grassroots networks, and exacerbate already existing issues of hyper-partisanship and media distrust. The massive quantity of digital disinformation messages produced and the reliance on surveillance to improve the effectiveness of the disinformation campaign further highlight why state-sponsored disinformation campaigns such as the Internet Research Agency's campaign toward the United States are highly concerning.

Though this essay has focused on Russia's Internet Research Agency as a case, the strategies employed by the IRA in U.S. social media demonstrate what over forty countries around the world can do. While disinformation campaigns vary by their goals and strategies, the IRA's perceived effectiveness, particularly in the United States during the 2016 election, has inspired other countries to use similar tactics for the mass production of disinformation (Martin et al. 2019). This trend should be highly concerning to communication and international relations scholars: if there is nothing to disincentivize countries from creating and maintaining disinformation campaigns, governments will continue to exploit media platforms with the intent of misleading domestic and foreign audiences. This phenomenon has grave consequences for the health of democratic countries.

Any government's use of disinformation campaigns and teams to target a foreign audience is explicitly antithetical to healthy international norms between countries, represents an overt violation of "Westphalian sovereignty," and contradicts good international citizenship. Using resources mainly available to nation-states, governments are capable of producing massive amounts of disinformation that artificially diminish the quality of political discourse around the world. State-sponsored disinformation campaigns also highlight the continued significance of real-world hierarchies in digital communication. Yes, the Internet has democratized who can become gatekeepers and information amplifiers. But the Internet is also as exploitable by political actors as any other platform, making it easier for governments to maintain authoritarian control over their states and to influence other states.

Several law briefs have noted that use of disinformation troll armies by a government is not explicitly illegal in terms of international laws, though their use during elections is deplorable as a violation of state sovereignty (Nicholas 2018; Rodriguez 2019). Solutions have ranged from increasing media literacy to developing a government program to combat state-sponsored disinformation, to holding technological companies responsible for disinformation on their platforms. One limitation of these strategies, taken individually, is that they put the onus on the individuals and groups being affected by the disinformation, rather than criticizing the country engaging in disinformation production.

On the other hand, it is exceedingly difficult—if not impossible—to stop countries from using disinformation tactics altogether, given that disinformation campaigns are a low-cost strategy with a potentially large impact on democratic institutions. Most major superpowers, including the United States, China, and (as discussed in this essay) Russia, maintain troll armies. As Nicolas (2018) notes, national and global attempts to combat state-sponsored disinformation will require multiple strategies, including the establishment of top-down norms that discourage countries from managing or supporting disinformation actors and strategies and bottom-up norms that help countries identify and combat troll armies that are active in their democratic institutions. One potentially fruitful top-down endeavor may be to pass a United Nations resolution that, while not binding, could build international norms against these tactics. In addition to media literacy, political and economic education might provide all citizens with a basic understanding of social systems.

However, we may have to accept that social media platforms—as with all political communication systems—are prone to exploitation and abuse by foreign actors. This was true of communication systems prior to the digital era, and it is likely to remain true. Our goal, as researchers, scholars, teachers, and global citizens, should be to find ways to minimize the amount of disinformation in our political discourse as much as possible by studying the strategies employed by state actors and by denouncing the use of disinformation campaigns.

Abang, O., and E. E. Okon. 2018. "Fake News, Misinformation Disinformation and Deception as Communication Channels of Democratic Governance in Nigeria." *International Journal of Integrative Humanism* 9: 135–43.

Abrams, S. 2016. "Beyond Propaganda: Soviet Active Measures in Putin's Russia." *Connections* 15: 5–31. www.jstor.org/stable/26326426.

Al-Khateeb, S., M. N. Hussain, and N. Agarwal. 2019. "Leveraging Social Network Analysis and Cyber Forensics Approaches to Study Cyber Propaganda Campaigns." In T. Özyer, S. Bakshi, and R. Alhajj., eds. *Social Networks and Surveillance for Society*, 19–42. Springer.

Badawy, A., E. Ferrara, and K. Lerman. 2018. "Analyzing the Digital Traces of Political Manipulation: The 2016 Russian Interference Twitter Campaign." August. Presented at IEEE/ACM International Conference on Advances in Social Networks Analysis and Mining (ASONAM), 258–65. IEEE.

Bail, C. A., B. Guay, E. Maloney, A. Combs, D. S. Hillygus, F. Merhout, D. Freelon, and A. Volfovsky. 2020. "Assessing the Russian Internet Research Agency's Impact on the Political Attitudes and Behaviors of American Twitter Users in Late 2017." *Proceedings of the National Academy of Sciences* 117: 243–50.

Bastos, M., and J. Farkas. 2019. "'Donald Trump Is My President!': The Internet Research Agency Propaganda Machine." *Social Media + Society* 5 (3): 1–13. doi.10.1177/2056305119865466.

Baym, N. K. 2013. "Data Not Seen: The Uses and Shortcomings of Social Media Metrics." *First Monday* 18 (10).

Bennett, W., and S. Livingston. 2018. "The Disinformation Order: Disruptive Communication and the Decline of Democratic Institutions." *European Journal of Communication* 33: 122–39. doi.10.1177/0267323118760317.

Bittman, L. 1981. "Soviet Bloc 'Disinformation' and Other 'Active Measures.'" In R. Pfaltzgraff, U. Ra'anan, and W. Milberg, eds., *Intelligence Policy and National Security,* 212–28. Palgrave Macmillan. doi.10.1080/08850609008435142.

———. (1990). "The Use of Disinformation by Democracies." *International Journal of Intelligence and Counter Intelligence* 4 (2): 243–61.

Blevins, J. L., E. Edgerton, D. P. Jason, and J. J. Lee. 2021. "Shouting into the Wind: Medical Science Versus 'BS' in the Twitter Maelstrom of Politics and Misinformation about Hydroxchloroquine." *Social Media + Society* 7 (2): 1–14.

Boghardt, T. 2009. "Soviet Bloc Intelligence and Its AIDS Disinformation Campaign." *Studies in Intelligence* 53 (4): 1–24. upload.wikimedia.org/wikipedia/commons/b/b6/Operation_INFEKTION_-_Soviet_Bloc_Intelligence_and_Its_AIDS_Disinformation_Campaign.pdf.

Bradshaw, S., and P. N. Howard. 2018. "Challenging Truth and Trust: A Global Inventory of Organized Social Media Manipulation." *Oxford Internet Institute, Programme on Democracy & Technology.* demtech.oii.ox.ac.uk/research/posts/challenging-truth -and-trust-a-global-inventory-of-organized-social-media-manipulation/.

———. 2019. "The Global Disinformation Order: 2019 Global Inventory of Organized Social Media Manipulation." digitalcommons.unl.edu/cgi/viewcontent.cgi?article =1209&context=scholcom.

Collins, B. 2017. "This Guy Tricks Pro-Trump Media into Confusing Every Campaign Rally for the 2016 Cavaliers Championship Game." August 23. *Daily Beast.* www .thedailybeast.com/this-guy-tricks-pro-trump-media-into-confusing-every -campaign-rally-for-the-2016-cavaliers-championship-parade.

Crosset, V., S. Tanner, and A. Campana. 2019. "Researching Far Right Groups on Twitter: Methodological Challenges 2.0." *New Media and Society* 21 (4): 939–61. doi.10.1177 /1461444818817306.

Dawson, A., and M. Innes. 2019. "How Russia's Internet Research Agency Built Its Disinformation Campaign." *Political Quarterly* 90 (2): 245–56. doi.10.1111/1467 -923X.12690.

de Haldevang, M. 2017. "Russia's Troll Factory Also Paid 100 Activists in the U.S." *Quartz.* qz.com/1104195/russian-political-hacking-the-internet-research-agency -troll-farm-by-the-numbers/.

de Lame, D. 2005. "Re-Imagining Rwanda: Conflict, Survival and Disinformation in the Late Twentieth Century." *American Anthropologist* 107 (1): 161–62. doi.10.1525 /aa.2005.107.1.161.

Doherty, M. 1994. "Black Propaganda by Radio: The German Concordia Broadcasts to Britain 1940–1941." *Historical Journal of Film, Radio and Television* 14 (2): 167–97. doi.10.1080/01439689400260141.

Doroshenko, L., and J. Lukito. 2019. "Trollfare: Russia's Disinformation Campaign during Military Conflict in Ukraine." August 8. Presented to 2019 International Communication Division at conference of Association for Education in Journalism and Mass Communication, Toronto.

Etudo, U., V. Y. Yoon, and N. Yaraghi. 2019. "From Facebook to the Streets: Russian Troll Ads and Black Lives Matter Protests." January. In *Proceedings of the 52nd Hawaii International Conference on System Sciences.* scholarspace.manoa.hawaii. edu/items/f11deabc-95b0-4d59-9412-2b01761dd189.

Ferreira, R. G. 2008. "The CIA and Jacobo Arbenz: History of a Disinformation Campaign." *Journal of Third World Studies* 25 (2): 59–81. doi.10.2307/45194479.

Frankfurt, H. G. 2005. *On Bullshit.* Princeton University Press.

Freelon, D., and C. Wells. 2020. "Disinformation as Political Communication." *Political Communication* 37 (2): 145–56. doi.10.1080/10584609.2020.1723755.

Freelon, D., M. Bossetta, C. Wells, J. Lukito, Y. Xia, and K. Adams. 2020. "Black Trolls Matter: Racial and Ideological Asymmetries in Social Media Disinformation." *Social Science Computer Review* 40 (3): 1–19. doi.10.1177/0894439320914853.

Gallacher, J. D., V. Barash, P. N. Howard, and J. Kelly. 2018. "Junk News on Military Affairs and National Security: Social Media Disinformation Campaigns against U.S. Military Personnel and Veterans." arXiv preprint. arXiv:1802.03572.

Garner, G. 2010. "Case studies in exploiting terrorist group divisions with disinformation and divisive/black propaganda." *Journal of Terrorism Research* 1: 3–14.

Gelders, D., and Ø. Ihlen. 2010. "Government Communication about Potential Policies: Public Relations, Propaganda or Both?" *Public Relations Review* 36 (1): 59–62. doi.10.1016/j.pubrev.2009.08.012.

Godson, R., and R. Shultz. 1985. "Soviet Active Measures: Distinctions and Definitions." *Defense Analysis* 1 (2): 101–10. doi.10.1080/07430178508405191.

Gray, T., and B. Martin. 2007. "Backfires: White, Black and Grey." *Journal of Information Warfare* 6 (1): 7–16. www.jstor.org/stable/26503465.

Green, J. J. 2018. "Tale of a Troll: Inside the 'Internet Research Agency' of Russia." September 17. *WTOP News.* wtop.com/j-j-green-national/2018/09/tale-of-a-troll -inside-the-internet-research-agency-in-russia/.

Harris, D. 2017. "Former Employees Expose Inner Workings of Russian Troll Farm." November 1. *ABC News.* abcnews.go.com/International/employees-expose -workings-russian-troll-farm/story?id=50866368.

Holtmann, P. 2013. "Countering al-Qaeda's Single Narrative." *Perspectives on Terrorism* 7(2): 141–46.

House Intelligence Committee. 2017. "Exhibit B [List of IRA-linked Twitter accounts]." democrats-intelligence.house.gov/uploadedfiles/exhibit_b.pdf.

Huckin, T. 2016. "Propaganda Defined." In Bazerman, ed., *Propaganda and rhetoric in democracy: History, theory, analysis*, 118–36. Southern Illinois University Press.

Imamverdiyev, Y. 2016. "Social Media and Security Concerns." *Problems of Information Society* 7 (2): 18–23. doi.10.25045/jpis.v07.i2.02.

Jamieson, K. H. 2018. *Cyberwar: How Russian Hackers and Trolls Helped Elect a President: What We Don't, Can't, and Do Know.* Oxford University Press.

Keller, F. B., D. Schoch, S. Stier, and J. Yang. 2020. "Political Astroturfing on Twitter: How to Coordinate a Disinformation Campaign." *Political Communication* 37(2): 256–80. doi.10.1080/1058409.2019.1661888.

Kim, D., T. Graham, Z. Wan, and M. A. Rizoiu. 2019. "Analysing User Identity Via Time-Sensitive Semantic Edit Distance (T-SED): A Case Study of Russian Trolls on Twitter." *Journal of Computational Social Science* 2(2): 331–51.

Krasner, S. D. 2001. "Rethinking the Sovereign State Model." *Review of International Studies* 27 (5): 17–42. doi.10.1017/S0260210501008014.

Krueger, B. S. 2005. "Government Surveillance and Political Participation on the Internet." *Social Science Computer Review* 23 (4): 439–52. doi.10.1177/0894439305278871.

Linvill, D. L., and P. L. Warren. 2020. "Troll Factories: Manufacturing Specialized Disinformation on Twitter." *Political Communication* 37 (4): 447–67. doi.10.1080/10 584609.2020.1718257.

Llewellyn, C., L. Cram, A. Favero, and R. L. Hill. 2018. "Russian Troll Hunting in a Brexit Twitter Archive." May. In *Proceedings of the 18th ACM/IEEE on Joint Conference on Digital Libraries*, 361–62. dl.acm.org/doi/abs/10.1145/3197026.3203876.

Loui, R., and W. Hope. 2017. "Information Warfare Amplified by Cyberwarfare and Hacking the National Knowledge Infrastructure." November. In *2017 IEEE 15th Intl Conf on Dependable, Autonomic and Secure Computing*, 280–83. IEEE.

Lukito, J. 2020. "Coordinating a Multi-Platform Disinformation Campaign: Internet Research Agency Activity on Three U.S. Social Media Platforms, 2015 to 2017." *Political Communication* 37 (2): 238–55.

———, Suk, J., Y. Zhang, L. Doroshenko, S. Kim, M. H. Su, Y. Xia, D. Freelon, and C. Wells 2020. "The Wolves in Sheep's Clothing: How Russia's Internet Research Agency Tweets Appeared in U.S. News as Vox Populi." *International Journal of Press/Politics* 25 (2): 196–216. doi.10.1177/1940161211989515.

Martin, D. A., J. N. Shapiro, and M. Nedashkovskaya. 2019. "Recent Trends in Online Foreign Influence Efforts." *Journal of Information Warfare* 18: 15–48.

Martin, L. J. 1982. "Disinformation: An Instrumentality in the Propaganda Arsenal." *Political Communication* 2 (1): 47–64. doi.10.1080/10584609.1982.9962747.

McLaverty, P. 2002. "Civil Society and Democracy." *Contemporary Politics* 8 (4): 303–18. doi.10.1080/1356770216068.

Mejias, U. A., and N. E. Vokuev. 2017. "Disinformation and the Media: The Case of Russia and Ukraine." *Media, Culture and Society* 39 (7): 1027–42. doi.10.1177 /0163443716686672.

Melissen, J. 2011. *Beyond the New Public Diplomacy*. Netherlands Institute of International Relations. www.clingendael.org/sites/default/files/pdfs/20111014_cdsp_ paper_jmelissen.pdf.

Michaelsen, M., and M. Glasius. 2018. "Authoritarian Practices in the Digital Age— Introduction." *International Journal of Communication* 12: 1–7.

Mueller, R. S. 2019. *Report on the Investigation into Russian Interference in the 2016 Presidential Election*, vol. 1. 28 C.F.R. §600.8(c). Washington, DC: U.S. Department of Justice. www.justice.gov/storage/report.pdf.

Nicolas, A. C. 2018. "Taming the Trolls: The Need for an International Legal Framework to Regulate State Use of Disinformation on Social Media." *Geo. LJ Online* 107: 36.

Oates, S. 2017. "Kompromat Goes Global? Assessing a Russian Media Tool in the United States." *Slavic Review* 76 (S1): S57–S65.

Orr, C. 2018. "Russia's Troll Factory Just Launched a New Website Targeting Americans." June 5. *Arc Digital*. arcdigital.media/russias-troll-factory-just-launched-a -new-website-targeting-americans-cbacdcf3e842.

Pearce, K. E. 2015. "Democratizing Kompromat: The Affordances of Social Media for State-Sponsored Harassment." *Information, Communication & Society* 18 (10): 1158–74.

Rizoiu, M., T. Graham, R. Zhang, Y. Zhang, R. Ackland, and L. Xie. 2018. "#DebateNight: The Role and Influence of Socialbots on Twitter during the 1st 2016 U.S. Presidential Debate." In *Twelfth International AAAI Conference on Web and Social Media*.

Rodriguez, M. 2019. "Disinformation Operations Aimed at (Democratic) Elections in the Context of Public International Law: The Conduct of the Internet Research Agency during the 2016 U.S. Presidential Election." *International Journal of Legal Information* 47 (3): 149–97.

Romerstein, H. 2001. "Disinformation as a KGB Weapon in the Cold War." *Journal of Intelligence History* 1 (1): 54–67. doi.10.1080/16161262.2001.10555046.

Ruck, D. J., N. M. Rice, J. Borycz, and R. A. Bentley. 2019. "Internet Research Agency Twitter Activity Predicted 2016 U.S. Election Polls." *First Monday* 24 (7).

Sanovich, S. 2017. "Computational Propaganda in Russia: The Origins of Digital Misinformation." *Computational Propaganda Research Project*. demtech.oii.ox.ac.uk /wp-content/uploads/sites/12/2017/06/Comprop-Russia.pdf.

Santini, R. M., D. Salles, G. Tucci, F. Ferreira, and F. Grael. 2020. "Making Up Audience: Media Bots and the Falsification of the Public Sphere." *Communication Studies* 71 (3): 1–22. doi.10.1080/10510974.2020.1735466.

Seddon, M. 2014. "Documents Show How Russia's Troll Army Hit America." October 17. *BuzzFeed News*. www.buzzfeednews.com/article/maxseddon/documents-show-how-russias-troll-army-hit-america.

Selvage, D. 2019. "Operation 'Denver': The East German Ministry of State Security and the KGB's AIDS Disinformation Campaign, 1985–1986 (Part 1)." *Journal of Cold War Studies* 21 (4): 71–123.

Shah, F. 2011. "Propaganda and Warfare in Cyber World." *Defense Journal* 15 (1–2): 79.

Sinclair, N. 2016. "Old Generation Warfare: The Evolution—Not Revolution—of the Russian Way of Warfare." *Military Review* 96 (3): 8.

Spangher, A., G. Ranade, B. Nushi, A. Fourney, and E. Horvitz. 2020. "Characterizing Search-Engine Traffic to Internet Research Agency Web Properties." In *Proceedings of The Web Conference 2020*, 2253–63.

Speier, H. 1948. "The Future of Psychological Warfare." *Public Opinion Quarterly* 12 (1): 5–18.

Tandoc, E. C. Jr., and R. J. Thomas. 2014. "The Ethics of Web Analytics: Implications of Using Audience Metrics in News Construction." *Digital Journalism* 3 (2): 243–58. doi.10.1080/21670811.2014.909122

United States of America v. Internet Research Agency. 18 U.S.C. §§ 2, 371, 1349, 1028A (2018). www.justice.gov/d9/fieldable-panel-panes/basic-panes/attachments /2018/02/16/internet_research_agency_indictment.pdf.

Wardle, C. 2018. "The Need for Smarter Definitions and Practical, Timely Empirical Research on Information Disorder." *Digital Journalism* 6 (8): 951–63. doi.10.1080 /21670811.2018.1502047.

Woolley, S. C., and P. N. Howard (eds.). 2018. *Computational Propaganda: Political Parties, Politicians, and Political Manipulation on Social Media.* Oxford University Press.

Xia, Y., J. Lukito, Y. Zhang, C. Wells, S. J. Kim, and C. Tong. 2019. "Disinformation Performed: Self-Presentation of a Russian IRA Account on Twitter." *Information, Communication and Society* 22 (11): 1646–64. doi.10.1080/1369118X.2019.1621921.

Yang, X., Q. Yang, and C. Wilson. 2015. "Penny for Your Thoughts: Searching for the 50 Cent Party on Sina Weibo." In *9th International AAAI conference on web and social media.* ojs.aaai.org/index.php/ICWSM/article/download/14649/14498.

Zannettou, S., T. Caulfield, E. De Cristofaro, M. Sirivianos, G. Stringhini, and J. Blackburn. 2019. "Disinformation Warfare: Understanding State-Sponsored Trolls on Twitter and Their Influence on the Web." May. In *Companion Proceedings of the 2019 World Wide Web Conference,* 218–26. dl.acm.org/doi/pdf/10.1145 /3308560.3316495.

Zhang, Y., J. Lukito, M.-H. Su, J. Suk, Y. Zia, S. J. Kim, L. Doroshenko, and C. Wells. Under review. "Assembling Social Media Followings through Polarized Publics and Media: How Russian IRA Accounts Gained Influence in the 2016 U.S. Election Cycle." *Journal of Communication.*

Digital Platforms Are Downstream of the Regulatory State

• • •

DAVID KARPF

There is a fundamental tension driving how we approached misinformation, disinformation, and foreign propaganda in the 2020 election. The
tension can best be summarized thus: digital platforms are *downstream*
of the regulatory state. In the absence of functional regulatory bodies,
the digital platforms fill in as quasi-regulators of last resort. This is bad
for the platforms, bad for politicians, and bad for the public. The platforms are not well-suited to the role; they are not positioned to succeed
in the role; they ought not have such power. Yet they are left to play it
nonetheless. They are the last remaining available option. If the regulators will not do their jobs and set the boundaries of political speech, then
those decisions are relegated to Mark Zuckerberg, Jack Dorsey (replaced
later by Elon Musk), and Sundar Pichai. This is an outrage, but the outrage begins with governmental failure and then extends to tech-platform
misbehavior. It does not originate with the platforms themselves.

First, a Memory

It was June 2015. I had been invited to attend a daylong meeting of academics, practitioners, and technologists to discuss the near-term tra-

jectory of online political advertising. This was, in so many ways, the *before-times.* Donald Trump had only declared his presidential candidacy a week earlier. His presidential campaign was still widely viewed as a joke—the type of celebrity vanity campaign that provides a brief distraction in the early months of the far-too-long election cycle, before the serious candidates (Jeb Bush, Ted Cruz, Marco Rubio, Scott Walker) settled into the real primary contest. The meeting assembled a group of experts, none of whom had any clue what was to come. This was before troll factories, before Cambridge Analytica, before the *techlash*—a rising public mistrust of big tech firms that continues to this day. But in one important sense, the meeting was an *omen.* It set the stage for the years that have followed.

The meeting was billed as "a broad overview of online political advertising, what scholars know, what we would like to know, the perspective of political actors, and how future platforms and policies for online political ads might be improved." The subtext, I would quickly realize, was that it was a listening and brainstorming session between one of the major tech platforms (Google), digital campaign professionals, and digital campaign researchers. Google wanted to hear more about what was on the horizon for the upcoming election cycle. What were the most likely use-cases and abuse-cases? What policies should the company develop in advance? How should it prepare? Google wasn't looking to use our expertise to make more money or develop new products. It was conducting due diligence. It was requesting input from experts and stakeholders before crafting new internal regulations, treating its massive role in contemporary digital political communication with the seriousness that it deserves. This is good corporate behavior. I was happy to contribute my two cents, so to speak.

The most striking thing at the time was who was *absent* from the room. There was no representative of the Federal Election Commission (FEC). There was no representative of any government agency at all. Google was asking quasi-regulatory questions—questions that arguably fall within the jurisdiction of the actual regulators. But the regulators had not been invited to participate. What's more, there was no sense among the participants gathered in the room (me included) that this was an odd or noteworthy absence. The reality, as we all knew, was that the FEC had been deadlocked and dysfunctional for years—a broken agency whose own chair had taken to issuing public warnings about the commission's inability to fulfill its duties (Kroll 2015). The absence of a functional administrative state had created a vacuum. The tech platforms were left to fill the void as best they could. The listening session was evidence of Google taking its quasi-regulatory role seriously. If the FEC couldn't keep up with advances in digital campaigning, then the rest of us would have to do our best in the agency's absence.

I recall sensing as the meeting concluded that this could only end badly. Platforms like Google and Facebook have neither the standing, the incentives, nor the expertise to make tough policy decisions. They would face legitimate pressure and outrage from political parties and political campaigns. They would face less legitimate pressure from outside forces looking to bend and break the rules from unexpected angles. They would be left scrambling to amend the informal rules of American electoral campaigning on-the-fly. And they would have no choice but to do so—a failure to create and enforce rules is, in itself, a type of rulemaking. The decline of the regulatory state had left the tech platforms in an awkward, vulnerable state.

What Came Next

There is little need to rehash all that came next. If you are reading this volume, then you are doubtless familiar. Suffice it to say, no one present at that meeting in 2015 had thought to warn that the digital platforms should be on the lookout for political advertisements purchased with rubles. No one was fretting about sketchy websites masquerading as legitimate newspapers, buying cheap advertisements through Facebook and Google, and turning a hefty profit while injecting social media–friendly, completely made-up political stories into the online political conversation (Subramanian 2016). Conspiracy theories online were nothing new, but prior to 2016 they had not been nearly so viral nor so profitable (Karpf 2020).

Microtargeted digital campaign communications also played an especially prominent role in the campaign. Digital microtargeting is nothing new (Howard 2005; Kreiss 2012; Stromer-Galley 2013; Baldwin-Philippi 2015), but in the aftermath of such a hostile, closely contested campaign, the practice became the subject of extended public critical scrutiny. One digital firm in particular—Cambridge Analytica (CA)—was effectively cast in the role of "evil mastermind," having bragged openly before the campaign about its breakthroughs in "psychographic persuasion" and having boasted to journalists a mere week before the election about its digital voter-suppression efforts (Green and Issenberg 2016). The Cambridge Analytica scandal would become the subject of congressional hearings and a turning point in the techlash. Cambridge Analytica's role in the Trump campaign is often overstated—there is no evidence that the company effectively deployed psychographic profiling in the 2016 election, and its voter-suppression efforts were just reasonably well-targeted negative advertisements on Facebook. But the scandal nonetheless became a driving force in the platforms' efforts to manage digital political communication in 2018 and 2020.

In the aftermath of the chaotic 2016 election, Facebook / Instagram, Google / YouTube, and Twitter have faced increased public scrutiny, calls for regulation, and demands for increased accountability. Conservative politicians and media elites have stoked fears that the tech platforms are biased against conservatives, vacillating between demands that the platforms take a laissez-faire approach to extreme conservative voices on their platforms and threats of increased partisan oversight and regulation. Trump himself played a central role in these efforts, brazenly violating the platforms' content policies and effectively daring them to challenge a sitting president, while also holding public summits and private dinners with the executives of big tech firms.

The result has been a patchwork of company policies, frameworks, and initiatives. Each social media company has crafted its own rules for how, when, and from whom political advertisements would be permitted. Each company has adopted new policies for monitoring coordinated disinformation campaigns. Each company has promised to monitor and combat hate speech and harassment online. Each company has announced a new era of transparency and collaboration with academic researchers. Each company has then been (rightly) criticized for failing to live up to any of these promises. And throughout these messy, confusing years, the tech platforms have insisted they are trying their best, while critics have pointed out that the platforms are too big—that they ought not have this sort of authority in the first place.

Both are, in a sense, correct. The tech platforms did what publicly traded companies do—they sought to grow, to dominate their sectors, to defeat or acquire their competitors, and to lobby against regulations that would harm their business models. As Tim Wu notes in *The Curse of Bigness* (2018), the Federal Trade Commission effectively abandoned antitrust regulation in 2001, after the Bush administration chose to settle the lawsuit against Microsoft rather than breaking the company up. In the decades that followed, big tech got bigger, and regulators approved every merger and acquisition without batting an eyelash. Amidst the techlash, these tech firms have directed significant resources toward tracking, monitoring, and combating abuse on their platforms. But they have been inconsistent in their approaches, wielding an authority they did not expect in an arena they did not intend to dominate.

The limitations of this patchwork approach have become especially apparent in 2023. The world's richest Twitter addict, Elon Musk, decided to buy the company outright. He dismantled the entire trust-and-safety team, brought the worst offenders back onto the site, and attempted to paint the company's past efforts to limit malicious propaganda as a front for government-directed censorship. He also shut down researcher access to the platform. Zuckerberg and the leaders of other major platforms, reeling from falling stock prices, slashed their own trust-and-safety teams as well. It turns out the digital platforms viewed these efforts as a *nice-to-have,* not a *must-have,* all along.

The Conundrum of Platform Regulation

In the years following the 2016 election, it has become increasingly common for digital politics scholars, policy experts, and public intellectuals to call for increased platform regulation and antitrust enforcement. During a panel at the 2018 International Communication Association Annual Meeting, I offered an alternate perspective with a call for "responsible information monopolies" (Karpf 2018).

Let us start from the conclusion that many researchers correctly reach: Google and Facebook are effectively information monopolies. Run afoul of Google and Facebook, and your ability to be heard online is dramatically reduced. The two companies cannot completely silence speech they disagree with, but they can effectively muffle it so that it fails to rise above the din of online conversation. In the contemporary digital media landscape, Facebook and Google determine what types of online speech are *profitable*.

Many of my peers within the Internet research community reach this point as their conclusion: Google and Facebook are too big. They ought to be regulated. In the United States, it has become fashionable to call for aggressive regulatory oversight. The United States could adopt our own version of Europe's General Data Protection Regulation (GDPR). The FCC or the FEC or the FTC could craft its own regulatory frameworks or apply the existing frameworks that were developed for previous media giants. We could develop a Consumer Financial Protection Board (CFPB) for the protection of consumer data privacy. The government could revisit its competition policies and return to an era of aggressive antitrust enforcement.

The problem that I drew attention to, however, was that these calls for regulating the big Internet companies rested on a central suspension of disbelief. A CFPB for consumer data or a U.S. equivalent to the GDPR is a reasonable policy proposal, offered (circa 2018) amid unreasonable times. For those who were determined to see the government regulate or break up Google and Facebook, I had to ask: Which government?

This government? Which alumnus of the Trump golf–and–real estate empire ought to be put in charge of crafting responsible regulations for digital media platforms?

The creative fiction at the heart of "regulate the monopolies" arguments is that they pretend we are talking about a generic government. What's missing today is not a failure of imagination or a failure of courage from public intellectuals or government officials. The U.S. government is facing a crisis of competence—one that predates the Trump years but was dramatically expanded through his tenure, in well-publicized fashion. The Consumer Financial Protection Bureau, the State Department, the EPA, and every other agency were further hollowed out. I could not have predicted in 2018 how the emaciation of our administrative state would contribute to the spectacular public health failures of 2020. Suffice it to say that the country would have been better off if the Centers for Disease Control had the same independence and capacity in the Trump administration that it had during the Bush or Obama administrations.

This is an uncomfortable reality. It seems in one sense unprincipled to recommend that the Obama administration should have regulated, and the alternate-universe Clinton administration should regulate, and that the Biden administration ought to regulate, but then suggest a different course for life under the Trump administration. In an ideal world, we would have spent these intervening years crafting a sensible and responsible framework that constrains the behavior of information monopolies. But, as I warned my academic colleagues in 2018, we don't get to live in an ideal world. We are stuck living in this one.

A Nervous Information Monopoly
Is a Well-Behaved Information Monopoly

This dose of political realism about the state of the regulatory state circa 2018 led me to a complicated, semi-contradictory conclusion about platform behavior in the 2020 election: we could not break up the digital platforms in the near term. Doing so would cause more harm than good.

So we were left to rely on a mix of goodwill and rational self-interest of the platforms to try their best to regulate themselves.

The best we could hope for is that the tech platforms, hoping to avoid the next Cambridge Analytica scandal, and recognizing that (to quote Spider-Man) *"with great power comes great responsibility,"* would devote sufficient resources and develop and enforce good-enough policies to help us stumble through the 2020 and 2022 elections in a manner that left legitimate political campaigns and everyday citizens reasonably well equipped to participate efficaciously in the election.

The greater the legitimate public outrage at these tech platforms, the more clarion the calls for regulation or antitrust enforcement, the more likely it is that Google and Facebook will conclude that they must devote serious resources to keeping digital electoral communications as free and fair as they can. A nervous monopolist is a better-behaved monopolist. Yet this public outrage needs to be coupled, at least at some level, with patience. Regulating or unwinding the platform monopolies is a job for future Congresses and an eventually reinvigorated administrative state. (Significant progress has been made along these lines in the years since the 2020 election. The FTC is now pursuing aggressive enforcement actions. What it most seems to need is time and resources.) It is a medium-term solution that cannot directly address the short-term problem.

As such, even as a critic of the digital platforms, I often find myself empathizing with them a bit. We have asked them to take on regulatory tasks that they are ill-suited to. We have asked them to enforce their rules evenly, even against a Congress that uses such enforcement as a casus belli for taking aim at the platforms, in much the same way the previous president took aim against journalists as the "enemy of the people." We have asked them to create these rules, while also (correctly) lambasting them for being the arbiters of what types of speech will be heard online—a role that they ought not occupy.

I would not want to be one of the people charged with developing and enforcing these policies for Google or Facebook. Seeing, in the past year, how Elon Musk's Twitter has turned on the former employees that took on this task, I can only offer sympathy. It is an impossible and thankless task. And yet it is also necessary and important, vital to the continued health of the republic.

The Gordian knot of a problem here is that digital platforms are downstream of the regulatory state. The regulatory state eroded in much the same way that Ernest Hemingway described bankruptcy— "Gradually and then suddenly" (1926). The platforms eventually became the regulators of last resort. They ought not play such a role, and they are not equipped to excel in such a role. We ought to be critical of their policy choices and selective implementation. We ought to question how and why they came to occupy such a critical and essential role in public life. But we also must make pragmatic plans for unwinding this state of affairs. It originated not from the platforms' unchecked zeal, but from the decline of the administrative state.

Regulating digital politics in future elections will be a chaotic mess, and responsibility for managing that mess will be navigated in partnership with the platforms themselves. It ought not be this way, but it is, at least in the short term, an irresolvable mess.

REFERENCES

Baldwin-Philippi, Jessica. 2015. *Using Technology, Building Democracy: Digital Campaigning and the Construction of Citizenship.* New York: Oxford University Press.

Green, Joshua, and Sasha Issenberg. 2016. "Inside the Trump Bunker, with Days to Go." October 27. *Bloomberg.* www.bloomberg.com/news/articles/2016-10-27/inside-the -trump-bunker-with-12-days-to-go.

Hemingway, Ernest. 1926. *The Sun Also Rises.* New York: Simon and Schuster.

Howard, Philip N. 2005. *New Media Campaigns and the Managed Citizen.* New York: Cambridge University Press.

Karpf, Dave. 2018. "The Infowars Purge, and Life among Responsible Information Monopolies." August 9. medium.com/@davekarpf/the-infowars-purge-and-life -among-responsible-information-monopolies-ddaa14f6cfo.

———. 2020. "How Digital Disinformation Turned Dangerous." *The Disinformation Age.* Ed. W. Lance Bennett and Steven Livingston. New York: Cambridge University Press. 153–68.

Kreiss, Daniel. 2012. *Taking Our Country Back: The Crafting of Networked Politics from Howard Dean to Barack Obama.* New York: Oxford University Press.

Kroll, Andy. 2015. "The Chairwoman Who's at War with Her Own Agency." October 13. *The Atlantic.* www.theatlantic.com/politics/archive/2015/10/the-chairwoman -whos-at-war-with-her-own-agency/440031/.

Stromer-Galley, Jennifer. 2013. *Presidential Campaigning in the Internet Age.* New York: Oxford University Press.

Subramanian, Samanth. 2017. "Welcome to Veles, Fake News Factory to the World." *wired* 24, no. 2. www.wired.com/2017/02/veles-macedonia-fake-news/.

Wu, Tim. 2018. *The Curse of Bigness: Antitrust in the New Gilded Age.* New York: Columbia Global Reports.

What Makes a Misinformed Tweet Viral?

A Computational Mixed-Method Approach

• • •

ITAI HIMELBOIM, DROR WALTER, AND YOTAM OPHIR

Political and Electoral Misinformation
in the Age of Social Media

Upon leaving the now-defunct journalism museum, the Newseum, in Washington, DC, visitors found themselves facing a prominent quote from President Abraham Lincoln on the wall leading to the exit doors: "Let the people know the facts, and the country will be safe." Indeed, the flow of timely and accurate information is a prerequisite for sustaining a democracy, where individuals have the right to participate in decision-making based on their knowledge, beliefs, and attitudes (Delli Carpini and Keeter 1993). Unfortunately, misinformation, rumors, and lies have been constant staples of the American political information environment since the early days of the nation (Schudson 2001). Even today, many Americans believe inaccurate news is a critical problem for the nation, and about one-third of them believe that "misleading stories on social media pose the biggest threat to the safety of U.S. elections." At the same time, many accept long-refuted misinformation, for example that President Barack Obama was not born in the United States.

Political misinformation can have a harmful impact on society at large, on the political system, and on the democratic process (Kuklinski et al. 2000). Citizens form their attitudes and beliefs based on available information (Ajzen and Albarracín 2007; Delli Carpini and Keeter 1993), and if a majority accepts misinformation as true, it could serve as the basis for political decisions that can turn detrimental (Lewandowsky et al. 2012). Importantly, misinformation is often resistant to correction and change. Studies suggest that, even when people accept that the information they were exposed to is, in fact, misleading and wrong, some still rely on it when forming attitudes and making decisions (Ecker, Lewandowsky, and Tang 2010). For example, in the political arena, Thorson's experiments exposed participants to negative information about top donors allegedly associated with fictitious candidates (2016). Her findings suggest that, even when participants were informed that the information was incorrect, the misinformation retained an influence over their attitudes toward politicians. Dubbing this continued misinformation effect "belief echoes," she concluded that, "even when citizens encounter, process, and accept the correction, they are not immune to [misinformation's] attitudinal effects" (18). These conclusions received ample support in meta-analyses (Walter and Murphy 2018; Walter and Tukachinsky 2019). At the time of writing, despite massive scientific attempts to find effective ways to enhance corrections and cope with misinformation effects (Cappella et al. 2015; Nyhan and Reifler 2010; Sangalang, Ophir, and Cappella 2019), misinformation remains an imminent threat to society and individuals.

Online Diffusion of Misinformation

While political misinformation is nothing new, the severity and prevalence of the problem were dramatically exacerbated by the Internet and social media. Of course, even credible media organizations sometimes release inaccurate information unintentionally (Lewandowsky et al. 2012), such as when attempting to keep stories "balanced" (Clarke 2008). However, despite occasional inaccuracies in mainstream media reporting (for example, in the coverage of the Iraq war, see Glazier and Boydstun 2012), mainstream media maintain mechanisms aimed at limiting misinformation, such as filtering and gatekeeping practices (Janowitz 1975), that tend to be severely lacking, and at times nonexistent, on the Internet and on social media, where content is often user-generated and its dissemination rapid and wide (Vicario et al. 2016).

These days, people get information about most topics from social media platforms, including Twitter (Fung et al. 2016), Facebook (Guess, Nyhan, and Reifler 2018), and even Pinterest (Guidry et al. 2015). Given the lack of proper regulation and gatekeeping, much of the information obtained from social media is inaccurate, misleading, or plain wrong (Starbird et al. 2014). Recent studies suggest that the prevalence of online misinformation is on the rise (Yuxi Wang et al. 2019). Yet many Americans prefer to rely on information they derive from social media even when mainstream media is considered more accurate (Johnson and Kaye 2015).

To better identify, debunk, and reduce political misinformation on social media, we should better understand what makes content online viral. The question of virality has occupied communication researchers for years. Virality is hard to predict, due to the immense amount of content online, and the role played by chance and serendipity. Nevertheless, researchers have identified factors that, on average, increase virality. Unfortunately, some of the factors often characterize misinformation, which could explain why vaccine misinformation, for example, is prevalent on almost all social media platforms, from Facebook (Burki 2020) to Pinterest (Guidry et al. 2015) to the extremist dark corners of the Internet (Walter et al. 2022). For example, people share information that makes them look good, smart, in the know, or important, traits often called "social currency" (Berger and Schwartz 2011). Messages are also more likely to get shared when they induce emotions, especially ones that drive people to action, like fear and anger (for example, Wang and Lee 2020), as well as content perceived as novel and surprising (Vosoughi, Roy, and Aral 2018). Finally, misinformation often benefits from being embedded within engaging narratives, making it both more viral and harder to debunk (Sangalang, Ophir, and Cappella 2019).

While much attention was given in recent years to the effects of message (Cappella, Kim, and Albarracín 2015) and network (Humprecht, Esser, and Van Aelst 2020; Vicario et al. 2016) characteristics, relatively little attention has been given to the characteristics of the individual people sharing the misinformation, and particularly to what makes an online user more or less likely to be shared by others, or "become viral." In this essay, we advance our understanding of the virality of misinformation online by suggesting a novel computational approach that measures the effects of social media "personae" (Walter, Ophir, and Jamieson 2020) on virality.

While the work by Walter and colleagues (2020) was dedicated to fabricated personae (that is, inauthentic users used for political purposes), here we suggest employing their linguistic method to identify thematic personae within distributors of misinformation on Twitter and to examine whether personae differ in their content's tendency to be retweeted. Specifically, we examine the effects of using categories of information in the user's profile, the short Twitter description written by users ("Bio"), identified automatically, on virality. Our first step is to explore the thematic personae used by users posting political misinformation on Twitter: *RQ1: What thematic personae do users who post links to political misinformation on Twitter belong to, based on their self-description (bio)?*

In the next sections, we introduce factors known to affect the spread of misinformation, introduce our own approach, and demonstrate its feasibility by using case studies (misinformed news links that went viral on Twitter). We conclude by discussing practical and theoretical implications for our approach.

What Makes Content Viral?

Scholars have been studying what makes people like, share, subscribe to, or reply to messages since the early days of social media. Most studies in this area focus on the relationships between users, the typography of the network, and message characteristics. Examining relationships between message creators and those who share messages, scholars (Fiore, Tiernan, and Smith 2002) showed that Usenet participants' perceptions of trust or respect for authors were positively correlated with the number of replies they received. Considering political similarities between user and source, studies (Adamic and Glance 2005) examined the political blogosphere, finding that bloggers prefer posting hyperlinks to other like-minded bloggers, a phenomenon known as homophily (Kossinets and Watts 2009). The identity of the source in relation to its retweeter could also successfully predict retweets (Zaman et al. 2010). As for message characteristics, Jones and colleagues (2002) found that shorter and simpler messages in newsgroups were more likely to attract user responses. Perceptions about content were found to influence engagement. For example, perceived features, such as usefulness, importance, novelty, tone, and exemplification, could explain content sharing or transmission on social media (Cappella, Kim, and Albarracín 2015; Keib, Himelboim and Han 2018; Kim 2015). Content combining text with images and videos (content modality) was found to be more likely to be shared than text-only posts (Pancer and Poole 2016).

At the moment, little is known about users' characteristics that make them more or less likely to be retweeted. (Characteristics are not the same as the relationship between the user and other users who share them.) Some studies have found that quantitative "social features," such as the number of followers, contribute to virality (Nesi et al. 2018; Petrovic, Osborne, and Lavrenko 2011), as well as authority indicators, such as the Twitter account verification symbol (Zaman et al. 2010). To this preliminary scientific knowledge, we add in this study the concept of thematic persona (Walter, Ophir, and Jamieson 2020). Thematic personae are "types of social media accounts that are consistent in their use of specific topics and discourse" (2). These could be identified using unsupervised machine-learning algorithms for text analysis (Soroka 2014; Walter, Ophir, and Jamieson 2020) able to identify recurring linguistic patterns in big corpora. For example, looking at the language-patterns use of Russian fake accounts during the 2016 U.S. elections,

Walter and colleagues (2020) identified nine coherent and consistent thematic personae. Based on the words a user used in tweets, they could automatically identify whether the character tended to talk about political issues (that is, pro–Donald Trump personae) or mundane ones (for example, a persona dedicated to online games and hashtags).

Literature provides wide support to the notion of similarities among user-personae of those who introduce content and those who share that content (here, retweet it). Two conceptual frameworks explain this: homophily, individuals' increased likelihood to interact with similar others; and selective exposure, individuals' selection of information that matches their beliefs, via interpersonal communication and news consumption (McPherson, Smith-Lovin, and Cook 2001). Himelboim and colleagues (2013) show that Twitter users are more likely to follow politically like-minded others, creating silos of politically homophilic users. Others (Shin et al. 2017) identify similar patterns in the spread of political misinformation, as homophilic follower networks helped rumor spreaders circulate false information on Twitter, and rarely played a self-correcting function. Political homophily also explains retweeting behavior (Wang and Luo 2018). Furthermore, Stewart and colleagues (2018) illustrate how bots take advantage of these homophilic structures to spread political misinformation. They found retweets of Russian Internet Research Agency (IRA) trolls' accounts to be largely contained within each network cluster.

While similarities between the characteristics of authors and users who share their content have been widely examined, what remains unexplored is their differences. For illustration, one would expect that conservative users would retweet content coming from other conservative users, but obviously not all conservatives are alike. Next, we examine whether "Content Introducers"—people who introduce misinformation into the network—differ from "Content Spreaders"—those who only retweet misinformation already existing in the Twitter environment. In other words, we examine whether thematic personae posting links to political misinformation differ from those who retweet them: *RQ2: Do users who introduce misinformation to Twitter ("Content Introducers") and users who only share it ("Content Spreaders") belong to different thematic personae? If so, how?*

When introducing misinformation on Twitter, especially via hyperlink, if content originated elsewhere, each user becomes a source of misinformation. However, not all are as successful in propagating misinformation, as determined by the number of retweets they trigger. The same type of misinformation is often introduced to the network by many users; some gain more retweets than others. As political misinformation is often very ideologically divisive, and as individuals tend to share information from like-minded others, how users present themselves on their Twitter profile may affect the likelihood that their content would be shared. Therefore, we ask: *RQ3: What characteristics of Content Introducers' profile description best explain misinformation sharing in Twitter networks?*

The Proposed Approach

This study proposes a data-driven approach to explaining misinformation diffusion on Twitter. Our approach uses a three-stage process. First, we use topic modeling to identify salient themes in the self-description of Twitter users who are spreading misinformation. At the second stage, we measure the pairwise similarity between all users in our sample and use these similarity scores to create a thematic network for these users. Lastly, we use community detection to divide this network into groups of users who share a similar mixture of themes in their self-description, which we refer to as thematic-persona groups.

While existing scholarship has supported the notion that users are more likely to engage with, including sharing content from, similar others, content-source characteristics that determine this similarity have been predetermined (for example, political leaning). Our approach is novel. First, it is fully inductive as it allows the user characteristics to organically evolve into themes, via their own profile descriptions. Second, while earlier studies classified user characteristics binarily (for example, conservative, liberal), the proposed approach ranks users on a range of organically generated themes, using topic modeling of the Twitter self-descriptions of users who posted misinformation tweets. Approaching user characteristics as continuous variables allows us to compare them and to explore which characteristics best predict the likelihood of misinformation-propagation success.

Methods: Data

Five political stories posted on the right-leaning Breitbart News Network website, Breitbart.com, that were determined to be mostly, very, or extremely misleading by credible fact-checking websites, such as snopes .com and politifact.com, were selected, based on their high shareability on Twitter. The stories are (1) "ICE Detainer Issued for Suspected Wine Country Arsonist in Sonoma Jail" on October 17, 2017, (2) "170 Registered Voters in Ohio's 12th District Listed as Over 116 Years Old" on August 8, 2018, (3) "DSH: 300 in Migrant Caravans Are Known Convicts, Gang Members" on November 2, 2018, (4) "National Immigration Forum Funded by Soros and the Left" on June 2, 2013, and (5) "Fact-Check: No, Fall River, Massachusetts, Was Not 'Built by Immigrants'" on January 30, 2018. By using these case studies, we do not try to capture any population of political misinformation on the web or on Twitter, nor do we attempt to capture a representative sample of users who share such information. Instead, articles were selected to test and illustrate the conceptual and methodological approaches presented here to better understand the sharing and spread of misinformation on Twitter.

The Crimson Hexagon (later Brandwatch), a social media analytics and data library, was used to collect all tweets that included either a link to these articles (including any short URLs used) or the title of the article, starting two days before the article was published, for a two-month period. Each of the five resulting datasets include all tweets, and for each its date, tweet content, author's name, handle, and self-description, where available. Only publicly available tweets were collected. Our initial number of tweets and retweets for all stories is 13,672. These tweets were authored by 11,198 unique users. We were able to retrieve the user data for 7,753 users. This is not surprising as accounts involved in such misinformation spreading are much more likely to be suspended by Twitter. Out of these users, roughly 90 percent, or 6,746 users, had a description line in their profile. These user descriptions were used to estimate the topic model.

Analysis

Analysis was conducted in three stages: (1) topic modeling of the textual descriptive data; (2) user-network generation from descriptive data similarities, and (3) community detection to discover and interpret close-knit thematic groups in the network. We elaborate on this process below. The full analysis code will be available upon request.

Topic Modeling

Topic modeling is a semiautomated, unsupervised method for the analysis of textual data, which uses a Bayesian generative approach to extract a set of topics from which the corpus under analysis could have been created (Blei, Ng, and Jordan 2003). Through an iterative process, topic modeling attempts to group together words that tend to co-occur and are assumed to be connected thematically. Thus, the term "topic" here refers to sets of frequency distributions of words that tend to appear frequently in the same documents. As every word in the corpus is associated with each topic, every document can be represented as a mixture of diverse topics (Walter and Ophir 2019). For example, the word "bank" can have different meanings in a topic about economics and in a topic about nature ("riverbank"). Topic modeling is inductive and unsupervised, meaning analysis is data-driven and is not guided by predetermined categories, and it does not consider syntax or word order ("bag of words" approach; see Blei, Ng, and Jordan 2003). For this essay's model we used Latent Dirichlet Allocation (LDA) with Gibbs sampling, tuning hyper-parameters to account for the corpus's unique features, being comprised of very short documents (Twitter bios).

The analysis took place in multiple steps. First, data were preprocessed, with hyperlinks, stop words, and numbers removed. We abstained from using stemming, following the recommendations described in Walter and Ophir (2019). Emojis and emoticons were automatically translated to text strings (such as "white heart"). For example, a locomotive emoji was often used after the word Trump to express "Trump train." Our algorithm translated that to "trump locomotive." For computational efficiency, we removed all words appearing in less than two documents (descriptions) or in more than 90 percent of all documents. The number of topics (forty) and hyperparameter ($\alpha = 0.05$) were chosen using a rigor process that optimized perplexity scores based on a tenfold cross-validation process. Finally, topics were interpreted qualitatively by a content analysis of top words and documents. (More details can be found in Walter and Ophir 2019.)

Comparing Content Introducers and Content Spreaders

Next, we scored each user in our data based on their use of each of the forty topics. This user-topic matrix was then split into two groups, "Content Introducers" (users who posted original tweets in our corpus at least once) and "Content Spreaders" (users who only retweeted content but never posted original tweets). As the distribution of topics' prevalence among users exhibited a long tail, we opted to use the more conservative nonparametric Mann-Whitney-Wilcoxon test to compare the groups (instead of t-tests). Due to multiple comparisons, we adjusted p-values using Bonferroni. All of these steps ensured a very statistically conservative process, one we believe is needed when evaluating significance levels using big data. Results can be seen in table 1, below.

Thematic Communities' Analysis

Next, we clustered the topics based on co-occurrence in Twitter bios. For each of the 1,632 Content Introducers we calculated the number of original posts they created (covariate in our models) and number of times they were retweeted (dependent variable). We then used cosine-similarity over the topic-document matrix to calculate the pairwise similarity between all Content Introducers' bios (that is, the extent to which each user's bio was similar to all other users' bios). This information regarding the relationship between users allowed us to calculate a network, where users serve as nodes and their similarities as edges. To reduce the network's density, we used backbone extraction at the significance level of $\alpha = 0.01$, keeping only significant edges. A fast-greedy algorithm divided the network into six communities, based on the use of similar language in bios. The meaning of communities was interpreted using qualitative analysis, similar to the one used for topics. The clustered user network can be seen in figure 1, below.

Lastly, we estimated the impact of membership in each of these six communities (used as a categorical variable) on retweets. Due to the large number of zero values in the dependent variable (that is, many tweets never got retweeted) and its extreme long tail distribution (only very few users got many retweets), we could not rely on ordinary least squares regressions. We compared potential models, including Poisson GLM models, negative binomial models, zero-inflated Poisson models, and zero-inflated negative binomial models and found the best performing model to be a hurdle model with a hybrid truncated negative binomial and binomial logit link model approach. The results of this model can be found in figure 1.

Findings

For all five news articles, we collected a corpus of 13,672 tweets, authored by 11,198 unique users. We were able to retrieve the user data for 7,753 users as many users deleted their account since publishing or were blocked by Twitter. Of those retrieved, 6,746 users included a self-description line (roughly 90 percent of users). Of these, 1,632 users posted original tweets at least once (Content Introducers) and the rest only retweeted others (Content Spreaders).

RQ1: What thematic personae do users who post links to political misinformation on Twitter belong to, based on their self-description (bio)?

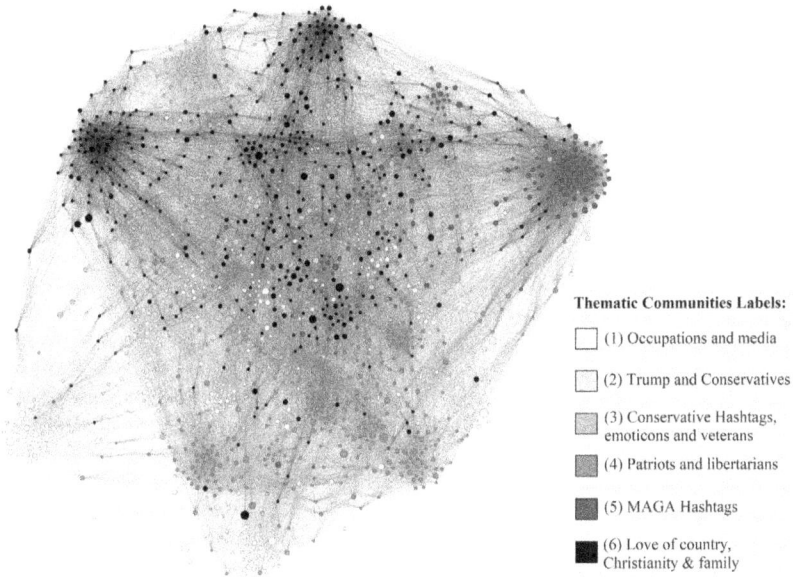

Thematic Communities Labels:

- ☐ (1) Occupations and media
- ☐ (2) Trump and Conservatives
- ▨ (3) Conservative Hashtags, emoticons and veterans
- ▨ (4) Patriots and libertarians
- ▨ (5) MAGA Hashtags
- ▮ (6) Love of country, Christianity & family

Fig. 1. The thematic community network for Content Introducers. Nodes represent users who tweeted (rather than just retweeted) at least once in our corpus (for one or more of the articles). Edges represent similarity in topic mixture of user description. Edges were reduced using backbone extraction at the α = 0.01 level. Node size represents the number of retweets users received for all their tweets in the dataset (with a spline for visibility). Variations in color represent community membership (see legend).

Our model of forty topics included a rich and diverse set of topics to which users referred when describing themselves. Included were topics relating to President Trump (for example, MAGA, #MAGA, Trump supporter), religion (for example, Christians, Jesus), Conservative issues (for example, liberty and freedom, patriotism, grassroots conservatism, constitution and conservatism, values and policies), and other political issues (for example, political affiliations, political officials, use of political hashtags, and anti-media and truth-seeking personae). Some topics were not political, including family-oriented topics (for example, proud father, proud mother), leisure and hobbies (for example, music, pets), occupations (for example, retired cop, a journalist) and Twitter functions (for example, one's Twitter "rules," such as "I'll follow those who follow me"). Other topics focused on emoticons, emojis, and hashtags. The full list of themes, including the top keywords that characterize each can be found in an online appendix. Figure 1 presents the clustered topic network.

RQ2: Do users who introduce misinformation to Twitter ("Content Introducers") and users who only share it ("Content Spreaders") belong to different thematic personae? If so, how?

Table 1. Significant theme differences between Content Introducers and Content Spreaders estimated using Mann-Whitney-Wilcoxon test and with Bonferroni corrected significance values

Topic Name	Significance (Bonferroni corrected)	Mean Difference (Introducer-Spreader)
Media Personnel	0.000004	0.018498797
Conservatives and Constitutional	0.000385	0.010316592
Occupations	0.000860	0.014050585
Political Affiliation	0.005651	0.005215288
Meta Twitter	0.011303	0.001941547
Grassroot Conservatism	0.017889	0.002770409
Anti-Media and Political Correctness	0.023723	0.007346904
Liberty Freedom	0.027687	0.003814889
Love and Proud	0.049763	0.003707969
Conservative Issues	0.049866	0.004069516

Note: All topics were more prevalent among Content Introducers

Nonparametric Mann-Whitney-Wilcoxon tests were used to compare language used by Content Introducers and Content Spreaders. Out of the forty topics, ten were found to be significantly different between the groups (see table 1). Notably, all ten were more prevalent among

Content Introducers than Content Spreaders, and no topic was used by Content Spreaders more than Introducers. It could be the result of Content Introducers being much more focused in their bios, thus using a more limited and pronounced set of specialized themes to self-describe their accounts. The full comparison can be seen in the online appendix. The following topics were more prevalent among Content Introducers. (See on-line appendix for full detailed lists of top words per topic. We avoid using examples verbatim to secure Twitter users' privacy.)

1. *Media Personnel* captures media professionals (for example, editors, talk-show hosts), using words like "radio" "host," "author," "writer," and "contributor."

2. *Conservatives and Constitutional* captures references to the U.S. Constitution from a conservative standpoint (for example, "Freedom loving Constitutional Conservative" or "Restoring Constitutional Principles"), using terms like "conservative," "constitution," "business," "rights," "small," "government," "constitutional," "freedom," and "liberty."

3. *Occupations* captures descriptions focused on work (for example, entrepreneur, consultant, artist, designer).

4. *Political Affiliation* captures mentions of political parties and movements (for example, Tea Party, Republican, "used to be liberal"); for example, users who detail their conversion from Democrat to independent or to conservative.

5. The *Meta Twitter* topic describes users who refer to Twitter's functions (such as direct messaging, following, unfollowing); for example, users who promise in bios to follow you back if you follow them.

6. *Grassroot Conservatism* includes references to grassroots organizations and activism, using terms such as #RedNationRisin and describing ballot initiatives.

7. *Anti-Media and Political Correctness* captures users expressing objections to certain issues (for example, "Skeptic and cynical," or

"not buying the BS from the mainstream") including terms such as "media," "tired," "libera," "lies," "fake," "enemy," and "corrupt."

8. *Liberty Freedom* includes fighting and pursuing justice, using terms such as "liberty," "truth," "freedom," "life," and "fighting."

9. *Love and Proud* often includes references to American pride and expressions of affection, often to the United States, but also to family, friends, or even religion ("love Jesus").

10. *Conservative Issues* captures references to issues such as gun control and abortion, using terms like "pro," "life," "Israel," "military," and "NRA."

RQ3: What characteristics of Content Introducers' profile description best explain misinformation sharing in Twitter networks?

After comparing Content Introducers and Content Spreaders, our next analysis focused only on Content Introducers. To facilitate RQ3, we clustered users into distinct "thematic personae" (Walter et al. 2020). The process (see Methods) resulted in six personae, each characterized by the use of a mixture of topics. We found the following personae: (1) *Occupations and Media,* (2) *Trump and Conservatives,* (3) *Conservative Hashtags, Emoticons, and Veterans,* (4) *Patriots and Libertarians,* (5) *MAGA Hashtags,* and (6) *Love of Country, Christianity, and Family.* Next, we examined whether belonging to a specific thematic persona influenced the number of times a user's content was retweeted by others.

Table 2 presents the results for the twelve models executed to test the relationship between the thematic persona of Content Introducer and the number of retweets they received. In each model we entered only one persona to the model (that is, without controlling other personae), while controlling for the specific news articles they wrote about (assuming some news articles received more attention than others). We conducted each analysis twice, with and without controlling for number of followers, to examine how much of the effect of thematic persona results from the number of followers associated with that persona.

Table 2. Results of Hurdle count and zero-inflated models on number of retweets received by Content Introducers

			Models without Followers			
	$M1$	$M2$	$M3$	$M4$	$M5$	$M6$
Intercept	-11.62	-13.81	-13.59	-12.04	-30.15	-10.67
Followers						
Article1	0.26	0.01	0.28	0.82	0.09	0.34
Article2	1.09*	0.84	1.105*	0.98*	0.86	0.96*
Article3	-1.39***	-1.46***	-1.42***	-1.25**	-1.19**	-1.49***
Article4	1.67***	1.17*	1.64***	2.31***	1.29**	1.62***
Article5	-1.14*	-1.41**	-1.12*	-1.06*	-1.21*	-1.30*
Comm1	0.092					
Comm2		0.65				
Comm3			0.14			
Comm4				1.13**		
Comm5					-1.31***	
Comm6						-0.72**
Intercept	-1.96***	-1.98***	-1.93***	-1.90***	-1.98***	-1.95***
Followers						
Article1	1.19***	1.18***	1.19***	1.19***	1.19***	1.19***
Article2	1.03***	1.03***	1.03***	1.04***	1.03***	1.03***
Article3	0.57*	0.58*	0.57*	0.58*	0.58*	0.58*
Article4	0.99***	0.99***	0.99***	1.00***	1.00***	0.99***
Article5	0.51*	0.51*	0.51*	0.51*	0.52*	0.51*
Comm1	0.10					
Comm2		0.21				
Comm3			-0.12			
Comm4				-0.26		
Comm5					0.25	
Comm6						0.00
Loglik	-2146	-2143	-2146	-2140	-2138	-2142
Df	15	15	15	15	15	15

* p < .05, ** p < .01, *** p < .001

Note: Count model coefficients (truncated negbin with log link).

Table 2. *(continued)*

| | Models with Followers | | | | | |
	M7	M8	M9	M10	M11	M12
Intercept	-18.05	-17.70	-17.13	-18.05	-18.73	-18.32
Followers	0.78***	0.78***	0.80***	0.79***	0.77***	0.80***
Article1	1.40**	1.63***	1.43**	1.53***	1.30**	1.27**
Article2	-0.69	-0.55	-0.77	-0.74	-0.73	-0.52
Article3	-1.02*	-0.97*	-0.99*	-1.03*	-0.85*	-0.82*
Article4	0.08	0.33	0.12	0.18	0.08	0.18
Article5	-1.79***	-1.59**	-1.81***	-1.75***	-1.70***	-1.57***
Comm1	-0.27					
Comm2		-0.41				
Comm3			-0.25			
Comm4				0.26		
Comm5					-0.58	
Comm6						0.62*
Intercept	-7.76***	-7.88***	-7.68***	-7.66***	-7.73***	-7.69***
Followers	0.72***	0.72***	0.71***	0.71***	0.72***	0.71***
Article1	0.91***	0.89***	0.92***	0.91***	0.91***	0.90***
Article2	0.66**	0.65**	0.66**	0.66**	0.65**	0.66**
Article3	0.43	0.46	0.44	0.44	0.45	0.45
Article4	0.90***	0.91***	0.90***	0.91***	0.91***	0.91***
Article5	0.26	0.27	0.28	0.28	0.27	0.27
Comm1	0.36					
Comm2		0.53**				
Comm3			-0.18			
Comm4				-0.14		
Comm5					-0.18	
Comm6						-0.08
Loglik	-1876	-1872	-1876	-1876	-1875	-1874
Df	17	17	17	17	17	17

* $p < .05$, ** $p < .01$, *** $p < .001$

Note: Count model coefficients (truncated negbin with log link).

Not controlling for number of followers, the *Patriots and Libertarians* (persona 4 above) was found to be positively related to number of retweets, while *MAGA Hashtags* and *Love of Country, Christianity, and Family* personae (5 and 6 above, respectively) showed negative association with number of retweets. When controlling for number of followers, only persona 6, *Love of Country, Christianity, and Family,* remains significant, and turns positive.

To elaborate, Content Introducers who belong to the *Patriots and Libertarians* persona (4) attracted more retweets, but only when not controlling for followers ($\beta = 1.13$, $p < .01$), as this group has more followers in general and their retweet performance turned is as expected, high. In terms of impact on misinformation distribution, then, they make the most impact, which is explained by the number of followers they tend to have. Users associated with *MAGA Hashtags* (persona 5) tended to have a relatively low number of followers. When not controlling for number of followers, belonging to this persona was negatively associated with number of retweets ($\beta = -1.31$, $p < .001$). When controlling for number of followers, this effect is nullified, signaling that their ineffectiveness may be due to a low number of followers. Lastly, persona 6, *Love of Country, Christianity, and Family,* was found to be negatively correlated with retweets when not controlling for followers ($\beta = -0.72$, $p < 0.01$), but the association turned positive when controlling for number of followers ($\beta = 0.62$, $p < .05$).

Discussion

The spread of misinformation on social media is a rising threat to democracies around the world (Lewandowsky et al. 2012). This essay applies a large-scale data-driven approach to identifying unique characteristics of users who spread misinformation on Twitter. Our method maps the ways these users describe themselves in their bios, distinguishes the thematic personae of those introducing misinformation on Twitter from those who only share it within the platform, and provides a methodological framework for predicting shareability of misinformation as a function of belonging to a thematic persona. To demonstrate the applicability of our new method, we applied it here to five examples of misinformation articles from Breitbart.com that were widely shared on Twitter.

We identified forty topics used in the misinformation distributors' Twitter bios based on the words and phrases users chose to define themselves with. Findings reveal a breadth of topics, from users highlighting their support for President Trump, to those focusing on their religiosity, activism, conservative beliefs (such as anti-abortion or gun control), and those describing themselves through their occupation or hobbies. As all users in our study posted articles from the right-wing conservative Breitbart, it is expected that all personae will be associated with or inclined toward the American right. However, the method provides a more detailed, fine-tuned understanding of their characteristics and the potential of different personae to create and spread misinformation.

Our results contribute conceptually and methodologically to our understanding of two categories of users who share misinformation on social media. We show that people who introduce new misinformation to the Twitter environment—Content Introducers—differ in their Twitter bios from those who only retweet others' misinformation—Content Spreaders. As expected, most users were Content Spreaders, only amplifying the misinformed arguments of others. In our case studies, ten of the forty topics in our model were more prevalent among Content Introducers than Content Spreaders. Specifically, Content Introducers associated themselves more with their conservative standpoints, political affiliation, and grassroots activities, media affiliation and mistrust in media, as well as their occupation. Notably, in this dataset no topic was found to be significantly more dominant among Content Spreaders, compared to Introducers. This could be the result of Spreaders' more diverse and less focused use of Twitter bios.

Finally, our results show differences in thematic personae's potential to spread misinformation, at least in the context of the five news articles examined. Following Walter and colleagues (2020), we identified six unique linguistic communities and found that one thematic persona, *Patriots and Libertarians,* best describes the group of Content Introducers that succeeded the most in misinformation diffusion. We demonstrate that their effectiveness results from their tendency to have more Twitter followers, an effect that still points to the persona's shareability, yet indicates that the effect did not come from the textual description itself but from other characteristics of the persona—in this case, sociability. Another persona, comprised of users who describe themselves through nonpolitical private information, here named *Christianity and Family,* held the strongest and only predictor for retweets in the face of the follower's control. That means that the language they use to describe themselves explains the number of retweets beyond the number of their followers, which they tend to have less of on average.

It should be noted as a caveat that we looked at only one aspect of virality, namely the nature of the users themselves and the way they describe themselves. Virality is hard to predict, and message, user, and network characteristics may interact with one another. Future studies may assess the relationship between the user characteristics studied here and other facets of virality. In addition, the current study used a small number of case studies to serve as proof of concept. We therefore do not argue that these personae will tend to be retweeted more across all political misinformation. Instead, we believe that shareability will be context dependent. However, future research using a much bigger and more diverse (such as conservative and liberal misinformation) dataset could find more consistent and reliable patterns and indicate, for example, whether more political personae are less or more likely to be shared when discussing political misinformation. While these are important theoretical questions, the main goal here was to introduce a new method for the identification of thematic personae who diffuse misinformation online, and to measure the association of belonging to these personae with one's ability to spread misinformation effectively on Twitter.

REFERENCES

Adamic, L. A., and N. Glance. 2005. "The Political Blogosphere and the 2004 U.S. Election: Divided They Blog." August. *Proceedings of the 3rd International Workshop on Link Discovery,* 36–43. doi.10.1145/1134271.1134277.

Ajzen, I., and D. Albarracín. 2007. "Predicting and Changing Behavior: A Reasoned Action Approach." In I. Ajzen, D. Albarracín, and R. C. Hornik, eds., *Prediction and Change of Health Behavior: Applying the Reasoned Action Approach*, 1–22. Lawrence Erlbaum Associates.

Berger, J., and E. M. Schwartz. 2011. "What Drives Immediate and Ongoing Word of Mouth?" *Journal of Marketing Research* 48 (5): 869–80. doi.org/10.1509/jmkr .48.5.869.

Blei, D. M., A. Y. Ng, and M. I. Jordan. 2003. "Latent Dirichlet Allocation." *Journal of Machine Learning Research* 3: 993–1022.

Burki, T. 2019. "Vaccine Misinformation and Social Media." *Lancet Digital Health* 1 (6): e258–59. doi.org/10.1016/S2589-7500(19)30136-0.

Cappella, J. N., H. S. Kim, and D. Albarracín. 2015. "Selection and Transmission Processes for Information in the Emerging Media Environment: Psychological Motives and Message Characteristics." *Media Psychology* 18 (3): 396–424. doi: 10.1080/15213269.2014.941112.

Cappella, J. N., E. Maloney, Y. Ophir, and E. Brennan. 2015. "Interventions to Correct Misinformation about Tobacco Products." *Tobacco Regulatory Science* 1 (2): 186–97. dx.doi.org/10.18001/TRS.1.2.8.

Clarke, C. E. 2008. "A Question of Balance: The Autism-Vaccine Controversy in the British and American Elite Press." *Science Communication* 30 (1): 77–107. doi.10.1177/1075547008320262.

Delli Carpini, M. X., and S. Keeter. 1993. "Measuring Political Knowledge: Putting First Things First." *American Journal of Political Science* 37 (4): 1179–1206. doi.10.2307/2111549.

Ecker, U. K. H., S. Lewandowsky, and D. T. W. Tang. 2010. "Explicit Warnings Reduce but Do Not Eliminate the Continued Influence of Misinformation." *Memory and Cognition* 38 (8): 1087–1100. doi.: 10.3758/MC.38.8.1087.

Fiore, A. T., S. L. Tiernan, and M. A. Smith. 2002. "Observed Behavior and Perceived Value of Authors in Usenet Newsgroups: Bridging the Gap." April. *Proceedings of the SIGCHI Conference on Human Factors in Computing Systems*, 323–30. doi.10.1145/503376.503434.

Fung, I. C.-H., C. H. Duke, K. C. Finch, K. R. Snook, P.-L. Tseng, A. C. Hernandez, M. Gambhir, K.-W. Fu, and Z. T. H. Tse. 2016. "Ebola Virus Disease and Social Media: A Systematic Review." *American Journal of Infection Control*. doi.10.1016/j.ajic .2016.05.011.

Glazier, R. A., and A. E. Boydstun. 2012. "The President, the Press, and the War: A Tale of Two Framing Agendas." *Political Communication* 29 (4): 428–46. doi.10.1080 /10584609.2012.721870.

Guess, A., B. Nyhan, and J. Reifler. 2018. *Selective Exposure to Misinformation: Evidence from the Consumption of Fake News during the 2016 U.S. Presidential Campaign.* European Research Council. www.ask-force.org/web/Fundamentalists/Guess-Selective-Exposure-to-Misinformation-Evidence-Presidential-Campaign-2018.pdf.

Guidry, J. P. D., K. Carlyle, M. Messner, and Y. Jin. 2015. "On Pins and Needles: How Vaccines Are Portrayed on Pinterest." *Vaccine* 33 (39): 5051–56. doi.org: 10.1016/j.vaccine.2015.08.064.

Himelboim, I., S. McCreery, and M. Smith. 2013. "Birds of a Feather Tweet Together: Integrating Network and Content Analyses to Examine Cross-Ideology Exposure on Twitter." *Journal of Computer-Mediated Communication* 18 (2): 154–74. doi.10.1111/jcc4.12001.

Humprecht, E., F. Esser, and P. Van Aelst. 2020. "Resilience to Online Disinformation: A Framework for Cross-National Comparative Research." *International Journal of Press/Politics* 25 (3). doi.10.1177/1940161219900126.

Janowitz, M. (1975). "Professional Models in Journalism: The Gatekeeper and the Advocate." *Journalism Quarterly* 52 (4): 618–26. doi.10.1177/107769907505200402.

Johnson, T. J., and B. K. Kaye. 2015. "Reasons to Believe: Influence of Credibility on Motivations for Using Social Networks." *Computers in Human Behavior* 50: 544–55. doi.org/10.1016/j.chb.2015.04.002.

Jones, Q., G. Ravid, and S. Rafaeli. 2002. "An Empirical Exploration of Mass Interaction System Dynamics: Individual Information Overload and Usenet Discourse." *Proceedings of the 35th Annual Hawaii International Conference on System Sciences,* 1050–59. doi.org/10.1109/HICSS.2002.994061.

Keib, K., L. Himelboim, and J.-Y. Han. 2018. "Important Tweets Matter: Predicting Retweets in the #Blacklivesmatter Talk on Twitter." *Computers in Human Behavior* 85: 106–15. doi.org/10.1016/j.chb.2018.03.025.

Kim, H. S. 2015. "Attracting views and Going Viral: How Message Features and News-Sharing Channels Affect Health News Diffusion." *Journal of Communication* 65 (3): 512–34. doi.10.1111/jcom.12160.

Kossinets, G., and D. J. Watts. 2009. "Origins of Homophily in an Evolving Social Network." *American Journal of Sociology* 115 (2): 405–50. doi.10.1086/599247.

Kuklinski, J. H., P. J. Quirk, J. Jerit, D. Schwieder, and R. F. Rich. (2000). "Misinformation and the Currency of Democratic Citizenship." *Journal of Politics* 62 (3): 790–816. doi.10.1111/0022-3816.00033.

Lewandowsky, S., U. K. H. Ecker, C. M. Seifert, N. Schwarz, and J. Cook. 2012. "Misinformation and Its Correction: Continued Influence and Successful Debiasing." *Psychological Science in the Public Interest* 13 (3): 106–31. doi.org/10.1177/1529100612451018.

McPherson, M., L. Smith-Lovin, and J. M. Cook. 2001. "Birds of a Feather: Homophily in Social Networks." *Annual Review of Sociology* 27 (1): 415–44. doi.10.1146/annurev .soc.27.1.415.

Nesi, P., G. Pantaleo, I. Paoli, and I. Zaza. 2018. "Assessing the ReTweet Proneness of Tweets: Predictive Models for Retweeting." *Multimedia Tools and Applications* 77 (20): 26371–96. doi.10.1007/s11042-018-5865-0.

Nyhan, B., and J. Reifler. 2010. "When Corrections Fail: The Persistence of Political Misperceptions." *Political Behavior* 32 (2): 303–30. doi.10.1007/s11109-010-9112-2.

Pancer, E., and M. Poole. 2016. "The Popularity and Virality of Political Social Media: Hashtags, Mentions, and Links Predict Likes and Retweets of 2016 U.S. Presidential Nominees' Tweets." *Social Influence* 11 (4): 259–70. doi.10.1080/15534510.2016.1265582.

Petrovic, S., M. Osborne, and V. Lavrenko. 2011. "RT to Win! Predicting Message Propagation in Twitter." July 5. *Fifth International AAAI Conference on Weblogs and Social Media* 5 (1). www.aaai.org/ocs/index.php/ICWSM/ICWSM11/paper/view/2754.

Sangalang, A., Y. Ophir, and J. N. Cappella. 2019. "The Potential for Narrative Correctives to Combat Misinformation." *Journal of Communication* 69 (3): 298–319. doi.10.1093/joc/jqz014.

Schudson, M. 2001. "The Objectivity Norm in American Journalism." *Journalism* 2 (2): 149–70. doi.10.1177/146488490100200201.

Shin, J., L. Jian, K. Driscoll, and F. Bar. 2017. "Political Rumoring on Twitter during the 2012 U.S. Presidential Election: Rumor Diffusion and Correction." *New Media and Society* 19 (8): 1214–35. doi.10.1177/1461444816634054.

Soroka, S. 2014. "Reliability and Validity in Automated Content Analysis." In R. P. Hart, ed., *Communication and Language Analysis in the Corporate World. IGI Global.*

Starbird, K., J. Maddock, M. Orand, P. Achterman, and R. M. Mason. 2014. *Rumors, False Flags, and Digital Vigilantes: Misinformation on Twitter after the 2013 Boston Marathon Bombing.* doi.10.9776/14308.

Stewart, L. G., A. Arif, and K. Starbird. 2018. *Examining Trolls and Polarization with a Retweet Network.* 6. Conference Paper, MIS2, Marina del Rey, CA.

Thorson, E. 2016. "Belief Echoes: The Persistent Effects of Corrected Misinformation." *Political Communication* 33 (3): 1–21. doi.10.1080/10584609.2015.1102187.

Vicario, M. D., A. Bessi, F. Zollo, F. Petroni, A. Scala, G. Caldarelli, H. E. Stanley, and W. Quattrociocchi. 2016. "The Spreading of Misinformation Online." *Proceedings of the National Academy of Sciences* 113 (3): 554–59. doi.10.1073/pnas.1517441113.

Vosoughi, S., D. Roy, and S. Aral. 2018. "The Spread of True and False News Online." *Science* 359 (6380): 1146–51. doi.org/10.1126/science.aap9559.

Walter, D., and Y. Ophir. 2019. "News Frame Analysis: An Inductive Mixed-Method Computational Approach." *Communication Methods and Measures* 13 (4): 248–66. doi.10.1080/19312458.2019.1639145.

Walter, D., Y. Ophir, and K. H. Jamieson. 2020. "Russian Twitter Accounts and the Partisan Polarization of Vaccine Discourse, 2015–2017." *American Journal of Public Health* 110 (5): 718–24. doi.10.2105/AJPH.2019.305564.

Walter, D., Y. Ophir, A. D. Lokmanoglu, and M. L. Pruden. 2022. "Vaccine Discourse in White Nationalist Online Communication: A Mixed-Methods Computational Approach." *Social Science & Medicine* 298: 114859. doi.org/10.1016/j.socscimed.2022.114859.

Walter, N., and S. T. Murphy. 2018. "How to Unring the Bell: A Meta-Analytic Approach to Correction of Misinformation." *Communication Monographs* 85 (3): 1–19. doi.10.1080/03637751.2018.1467564.

Walter, N., and R. Tukachinsky. 2019. "A Meta-Analytic Examination of the Continued Influence of Misinformation in the Face of Correction: How Powerful Is It, Why Does It Happen, and How to Stop It?" *Communication Research* 47 (2). doi.10.1177/0093650219854600.

Wang, Yu, and J. Luo. 2018. "The Great Division." ArXiv:1802.00156 [Cs]. arxiv.org/abs/1802.00156.

Wang, Yuxi, M. McKee, A. Torbica, and D. Stuckler. 2019. "Systematic Literature Review on the Spread of Health-Related Misinformation on Social Media." *Social Science and Medicine* 240. doi.10.1016/j.socscimed.2019.112552.

Wang, X., and E. W. J. Lee. 2020. "Negative Emotions Shape the Diffusion of Cancer Tweets: Toward an Integrated Social Network–Text Analytics Approach." *Internet Research* 31 (2): 401–18. doi.org/10.1108/INTR-04-2020-0181.

Zaman, T. R., R. Herbrich, J. V. Gael, and D. Stern. 2010. *Predicting Information Spreading in Twitter* 104 (45): 17599–17601.

Disinformation
and Latinx Social Media

• • •

CLAUDIA FLORES-SAVIAGA AND SAIPH SAVAGE

Beginning with the 2008 U.S. presidential campaign, political candidates such as Barack Obama have used social media platforms including Facebook, Twitter, and Reddit to engage citizens in political discussions. Since then, political leaders have used these platforms not only to mobilize the general public but also to raise awareness and get financial support for their campaigns. However, in 2016 the weaponization of social media platforms became evident. By then, the news media started documenting how "bad actors," also known as political trolls, were organizing within different social media platforms to spread propaganda. For that reason, we wanted to understand their forms of coordination in more depth. We were aware of previous work that had explored their extreme actions, and how their actions sometimes are related to culture (Summit-Gil 2016). We also knew that researchers had investigated how these bad actors created a myriad of accounts to deceive others and manipulate discussions online (Kumar et al. 2017). Detecting this has been crucial to better understand at scale this type of behavior (Kumar, Cheng, and Leskovec 2017). But for us, it was important to dig deeper and understand how these bad actors self-organized to cause harm. We know that these bad actors have to deal with the same challenges faced by other online communities, to sustain participation and to convince others to act collectively (Kraut et al. 2012). Even though their actions have given them a bad reputation, their success has allowed them to become problems for other online communities by undermining generalized norms of civility, which are essential for a democratic process. More recently, as the 2018 midterm elections approached in the United States, the news media started reporting on how these actors were targeting minority groups such as the Latinx community. Consequently, we needed to have a better level of comprehension of how they have been able to organize and mobilize others to be able to prepare for future elections. Understanding all this is paramount to contribute to the design of more inclusive civic media technologies.

In this essay, we present our research, based on two large-scale data analyses, that uncovered how political trolls produced disinformation and were able to mobilize action and engagement from people to spread their propaganda. First, we present our analysis of their behavior during the 2016 U.S. presidential election, where we uncover the tactics they used. What we found surprising about this research was the creativity of political trolls in using known mainstream tools to promote a shared identity and to motivate participation from others—for instance, using bots with a gamification component. Another finding was the use of conspiracy theories and their effectiveness to convince others to mobilize them.

Next, we present our research on how these political trolls targeted minority groups such as the Latinx community with disinformation, harassment, and computational propaganda before the 2018 U.S. midterm elections. In this analysis, we uncover how political trolls filled existing data voids with their own hateful content and disinformation.

We position our research in two main areas. The first one is related to the study of social media platforms as a medium to facilitate collective action. We refer to collective action as those efforts made by a group of people to achieve a common goal (Olson 2009). The second area relates to how these bad actors behave within the online communities in which they participate. First, we must understand that social media facilitate collective action by influencing people to respond in support of a cause. For instance, activists use various social media platforms to support diverse causes such as the Black Lives Matter movement. The Black Lives Matter movement is international, originating in the African American community, to campaign against violence and systemic racism toward Black people. Another example is the Arab Spring movements, which were a series of anti-government protests, uprisings, and armed rebellions that spread across the Arab world in the early 2010s. During these events, activists used a myriad of social media platforms such as Twitter and Facebook to influence people to take to the street to protest. These platforms ensured that they had reliable communication channels and created a snowball effect. Their conversations acted as social proof that they needed to encourage others to mobilize (De Choudhury et al. 2016). For this reason, we argue that social media provide a way to promote (or hinder) collective action by creating (or destroying) opportunities to communicate needs and to discover allies. Within social media, requests for help can unexpectedly be met with assistance, which enables positive feedback loops of reciprocal support that legitimize the action (Althoff, Danescu-Niculescu-Mizil, and Jurafsky 2014).

One concept we want to introduce is the concept of framing. In the social sciences, framing theory suggests that how we frame reality influences the choices individuals make about how to process the information presented to them. In this sense, a frame helps people to interpret individual experiences, and they use this frame to make sense of the world. For instance, some women have been using social media to frame the street harassment they experience, to then create effective campaigns for fighting back against it (Dimond et al. 2013). Through framing, social media platforms offer an opportunity to influence people's opinions and behavior. For social media movements, being able to frame the interpretations and meanings of a collective effort provides a way to legitimate or motivate the actions of the group. In politics, social media offers politicians an opportunity to influence people's opinions and behavior through framing (Matias 2016). For instance, Hemphill, Culotta, and Heston found that politicians actively use Twitter to frame issues by choosing topics to discuss and specific hashtags within topics (2013). However, less is known about the ability of deviant subcommunities to leverage social media and framing to encourage and support regressive, antisocial, or other disruptive online collective action. Previous work has analyzed these types of deviant actors from different angles. For example, Kumar, Cheng, and Leskovec studied patterns to predict users at risk of adopting trolling behavior (2017), and previously others focused on characterizing trolls' antisocial behavior (Cheng, Danescu-Niculescu-Mizil, and Leskovec 2015).

Other researchers had also documented the extreme acts conducted by these types of trolling communities (Shachaf and Hara 2010); however, we thought there was a gap in the understanding of the specific behaviors that bad actors used to succeed in their means. The consequences of their trolling efforts can have serious effects on the real world. For instance, individuals being targeted by members of these communities can experience a wide range of consequences such as depression, helplessness, anxiety, low levels of self-esteem, frustration, insecurity, and fear (Cheng et al. 2017; Coles and West 2016).

One deviant community is found in Something Awful Forums (SAF). Pater and colleagues (2014) studied how this community found sustained success even when deviating from common conventions and norms of online communities. For example, common practices such as abuse of newbies, public humiliation, and banning boring users actually work to strengthen connectedness and culture across the community.

Hacking, trolling, and other forms of cyber-disruption have taken on geopolitical dimensions as national governments invest in covertly spreading or undermining messages. One clear example is the "Fifty Cent Army." Named after a claim that employees make 50 cents per post, this army is thought to be a myriad of Chinese government-hired sock puppets that are in charge of disseminating messages praising the Chinese Communist Party on social media sites. It is estimated that this army fabricates and posts about 448 million social media comments a year (King, Pan, and Roberts 2017). Additionally, they rigorously enforced trolling-type messages against the limited dissent permitted (Han 2015).

Additionally, Bradshaw and Howard (2017) compiled one of the first inventories of government, military, or political party teams committed to manipulating public opinion over social media, across twenty-eight countries in their study. They found these types of teams to be a pervasive, global phenomenon, and not only do they target domestic audiences, but they also target foreign publics.

Various tactics of political trolls have previously been documented. One high profile case is the information warfare from Russia, also known as "dezinformatsiya." Evidence suggests that these disinformation campaigns are used by Russian intelligence to "sow discord among" and within countries to be hostile to Russia (Bertrand 2016). We want to understand how these deviant groups manage the same fundamental challenges of motivating and governing participation faced by traditional online communities in their own communities (Kraut et al. 2012).

Analyzing Subversive Behavior on Reddit: The 2016 U.S. Presidential Election

First, we present our research about one of the most active and largest communities on Reddit, a community-driven platform for discussion, news aggregation, and content rating that was created in 2005. This platform is composed of thousands of communities, also known as "subreddits" focused on different topics. People on Reddit can submit posts to a subreddit, and others can upvote or downvote the posts as well as comment on them. We focus on the subreddit /r/The Donald (T_D), which originated around the time Donald Trump announced his presidential run in June 2015 and received noteworthy media coverage during the 2016 U.S. presidential election.

Before its banning in June of 2020, the subreddit T_D followed Donald Trump's presidential campaign, his presidential win, and all of his actions and controversies in his presidential administration. T_D was labeled as one of the most active and largest political troll communities within

Reddit (Isaac 2020). This community has been highly controversial, and the hateful content posted there attracted numerous complaints. Researchers have documented that a substantial amount of the content originated allegedly from "alt-right" users, who also participated in racist, sexist, Islamophobic, and other antisocial subreddits (Lyons 2017). Users were in constant conflict with a number of other high-profile communities on the site and even the platform's administrators (Mills 2018). All these controversies made this subreddit a compelling community to understand by analyzing the dynamics behind the participants.

News media covered the efforts of this community to disrupt and harass various political actors, celebrities, and regular citizens. Our main focus is to analyze how these bad actors within T_D were able to sustain participation from outsiders and mobilize their participants to fulfill their purposes.

Examples of their tactics abound. Some of the most notable are those related to the creation of online repositories with memes and their consequential spread on social media. For instance, participants organized the use of satirical hashtags, such as #DraftOurDaughters to troll Hillary Clinton's initiative about supporting women to register for the military draft (Nelson 2018) or #ShariaOurDaughters to take Islamic ideologies to an absurd extreme. How it worked is that users created lists of the hashtags they wanted participants to use in their posts, as well as the prefabricated memes they wanted to spread. This way, participants did not have to invest a lot of time in the creation of the content (see figure 1, below).

Another example was how they organized boycotts of other platforms' content. For example, if there was a show on a streaming service that they considered opposed to their political views, they would encourage a boycott of the streaming service by inciting others to cancel their subscriptions (Thomas 2017; Kobb 2017). Another example was the boycotts organized against content creators. For example, they orchestrated one-star Amazon reviews for Megyn Kelly's 2016 autobiography (Crum 2016).

By mobilizing their members, they were able to flood the Internet with pro-Trump, anti–Hillary Clinton propaganda and harass Trump's detractors (Schreckinger 2017). We used T_D as a lens to understand how a political trolling community manages its own challenges around sustaining participation and mobilization at scale by analyzing more than sixteen million Reddit posts from this community from over 300,000 members, from June 30, 2015, to February 28, 2017.

Identifying Strategies to Mobilize to Action

In this analysis, we wanted to understand which tactics political trolls used to produce disinformation, and how they were able to mobilize action and engagement. To achieve this, first, we needed to identify those posts in which they were calling to action. We define a call to action as an exhortation or stimulus to do something in order to achieve a specific goal. One example of a post containing a call to action can be seen in figure 1. In this example, a participant created a post asking other participants to go to Twitter and retweet a specific post using a pre-generated image and using as many hashtags as possible from a pre-generated list for maximum exposure.

Fig. 1. Call to action.

To find these types of posts we first used a list of action verbs to flag posts with possible calls to action. Through this process, we identified 5,603 posts. Next, we hired three English-speaking college-educated workers to categorize whether each of the posts made a call to action or not. Coders would read each of the posts and determine if it was indeed a call to action or not, as it could be that the post had action verbs without trying to mobilize others.

Once we categorized the posts into "call-to-action" and "non-call-to-action" categories, we identified the authors of the posts and characterized them based on their "style" for making calls to action. We considered that each individual had a particular "style" for mobilizing others. Our goal was to group together individuals who used the same style. We then used a clustering method to group people with similar styles of calls to action. Specifically, we used a mean shift algorithm to discover different clusters of people, where each cluster represented groups of individuals with a particular style for making calls to action. Some of the characteristics we wanted our clustering algorithm to consider creating the groups were: if the call to action contained a link; if it mentioned a public figure or organization; if it used slang; if it used profanity; and the number of words. More details about this method can be read in our paper (Flores-Saviaga, Keegan, and Savage 2018). Using this method, we found three main clusters or strategies. We inspected each cluster in detail to better understand the call-to-action style being used. We named these strategies "Troll Slang," "Viral News," and "Historian."

In the "Troll Slang" style, some political activists appeared to be using slang in their online conversations, which supported their political beliefs. This appeared to be based on creating a collective identity, which might have solidified the identity of a group. For example, some Trump supporters called themselves "centipedes" and posted messages supporting Trump, "the God-Emperor," against "Killary" Clinton.

In the "Viral News" style, some political activists seemed to work hard on creating and identifying the content that was most likely to attract wide attention online. This facilitated large crowds to spread the content on other social networks easily. For example, some activists were in charge of creating collections of multimedia material for others to use along with the list of hashtags they wanted to promote.

Finally, in the "Historian" style, the lengthy posts resembled conspiracy theories. Participants provided historical context about the most relevant news stories that were circulating; however, they tweaked each story so that the focus of the story would be in their favor. In fact, we found that doing this seemed to be an effective way to drive participation from others, as those posts received the largest number of comments (see figure 2). This style might have facilitated long-term participation because it explained in detail the community's reasoning in the current political ecosystem and, thus, this might have encouraged others to take action. For instance, Trump backers compiled the top WikiLeaks revelations about Hillary Clinton, explained what they meant, and encouraged others to share them.

Understanding Engagement and Call to Action

A significant aspect of any call to action is to figure out if participants engaged with it. For our work, we defined engagement as people within the community commenting on the post that contained the call to action or if at least they upvoted the post. Within Reddit, if people think something contributes to the conversation, they upvote it. If they think it does not contribute to the subreddit in which it is posted or is off topic, they can downvote it. Therefore, we plotted the total number of upvotes (X-axis) and the number of comments (Y-axis) that each call to action received and color coded them according to their style.

Figure 2 shows that the "Historian" style appears to have continuously obtained a high number of upvotes and comments. However, the "Troll Slang" style occasionally managed to secure more engagement, although this was not common. The "Viral News" style, although it was rarely used, received a similar number of upvotes and comments regardless. The community usually engaged with this style less than with the "Historian" style, but it received more engagement than the "Viral News" style.

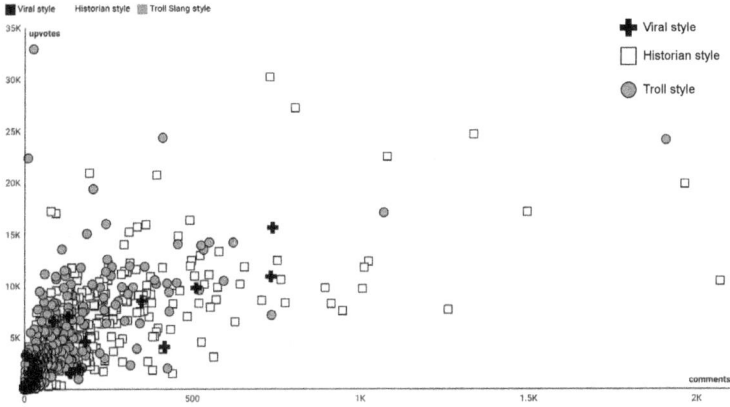

Fig. 2. Number of upvotes and comments that each call to action received.

Mechanisms to Sustain Engagement

Subversive communities such as T_D face challenges similar to those of any other online community. One challenge of any community is to keep participants entertained. One surprising finding is that T_D, to our knowledge, was one of the first to opportunistically use bots for creating an identity and engagement in a political context. Participants engaged with the bots to play games with them. Bots had a gamification component and were activated when participants used certain slang words or mentioned the bot. For example, in the "TrumpTrainBot," users are in charge of "moving forward" the "Trump Train." This bot increased its speed each time people used pro-Trump slang or replied to the bot.

Analyzing Subversive Behavior Targeting the Latinx Community

In more recent research, we were interested in analyzing whether these subversive communities were involved during the 2018 midterm elections. As most research has focused on how disinformation is targeting populations in general, we wanted to understand how online political discussions about minority groups such as the Latinx community were evolving on social media. The Latinx community is a major voting bloc as 27.3 million Latinxs were eligible to vote in 2016, a larger number than any other ethnic group of voters, representing 12 percent of all eligible voters (Krogstad et al. 2016). For this analysis, we collected Reddit posts related to Latinxs and elections from September 24, 2017, to September 24, 2018. Our Reddit sample consisted of only those posts mentioning words related to the Latinx communities and the midterm elections.

To achieve this, we manually compiled a list of keywords that were related to the Latinx community and the midterm elections. The list consisted of a variety of slang terms to describe Latinxs in a positive, neutral, or negative way. We identified terms that referred to each of the organizations and public figures that participated in some sort of way throughout the year prior to the 2018 midterm elections, from public officials to NGOs to opinion leaders (for example, names of candidates). We collected terms from a broad range of news websites that represented a variety of political views and inclinations. We made sure to include news reports that were in both English and Spanish. Then we used different combinations of terms to query Reddit. For example, we used combinations such as "midterms" + "latinos" or "midterms" + related slang for Latino; "elecciones medio término" ("midterm election" in Spanish) + "Latino." In the end, we collected 1,463 unique posts from 968 unique users from different subreddits.

Once we had this dataset, we wanted to quantify how many topics related to the Latinx community were being discussed over time. Therefore, we graphed people's posting patterns over time. The graph in figure 3 represents the temporal distribution of the content related to Latinx over time. Designing this graph helped us detect spikes of activity in the conversations relating to Latinx and midterm elections. Figure 3 illustrates the total number of Reddit posts made per day. The X-axis represents the date the post was made, and the Y-axis represents the total number of posts shared that particular day.

At first glance, we see that posts began to increase in February 2018. After conducting a qualitative analysis of the posts from that month, we

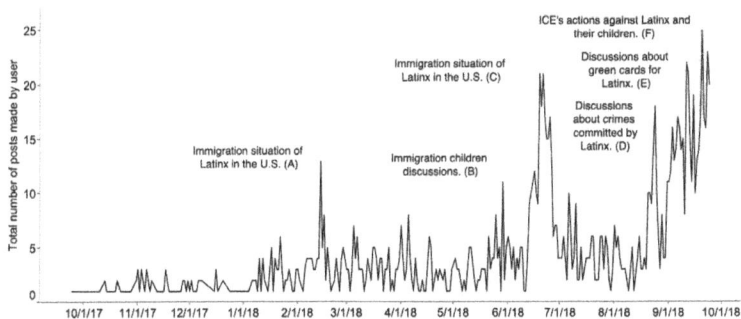

Fig. 3. Overview of people's behavior for content related to Latinx on Reddit before the 2018 midterm election.

realized the conversation revolved around the presidential primary elections that were taking place the following month in Texas, a state with a large number of Hispanics and Latinos of any race. They represent 38.2 percent of the state's population, as documented by the 2010 U.S. Census (Ennis 2010), and most of the discussions were about immigration issues.

The peak on February 14, 2018 (point A), coincided with the open-ended debate on immigration that began in the U.S. Senate the evening before and stalled when Democrats objected to the Republicans' first amendment, which would punish so-called sanctuary cities. Regarding this event, we saw evidence of conversations happening for days around that date. These conversations took place within mega-threads. A mega-thread is an extremely long discussion thread around a specific topic within a subreddit. These mega-threads seemed to gather a lot of participants to contextualize, explain, and discuss in detail their opinions about the topic being discussed. These types of online interactions in which participants explain in detail to others their point of view on a story are something we identified as effective for engaging individuals (Flores-Saviaga, Keegan, and Savage 2018). We also noted that participants engage people in discussions through AMAs. AMAs, also known as "Ask Me Anything sessions," are special threads where users can ask any questions they want to celebrities and high-profile individuals. These discussions appeared to have much more steady and continuous engagement. In contrast, we did not find any evidence of a mega-thread around topics that could have helped Latinxs to participate in political discussions or become involved in the election process, for example to guide them to register to vote.

The conversation during May 2018 shifted, and now it was focused on the treatment of children separated from undocumented immigrant parents at the border (point B). What was occurring was that adults who tried to cross the border were being placed in custody, and as a result, hundreds of minors were housed in detention centers and removed from their parents. This topic was widely covered by the news media and highly discussed on the platform. This discussion increased in the following months with a big spike on June 19, 2018 (point C). On that date, the conversations focused on how U.S. senator Bill Nelson, U.S. representative Debbie Wasserman Schultz, and state representative Kionne McGhee were denied entry to the Homestead Temporary Shelter for Unaccompanied Children, where twelve hundred immigrant children were being held (Smiley, Medina, and Daugherty 2018).

On September 11, 2018 (point D), there was a peak related to conversations about crimes committed by illegal immigrants and also posts discussing and encouraging others to support building the U.S. border wall. The top posts on September 20 and September 23, 2018 (points E to F), belonged to discussions about the policies Trump had proposed around immigrants, such as curtailing green cards for immigrants on public aid and the arrest by ICE of dozens of immigrants who tried to sponsor undocumented migrant children.

After seeing these patterns, we became interested in uncovering who were the main people driving these conversations. For this purpose, we identified the most active users on Reddit by finding those individuals whose number of posts was higher than three times the standard deviation. We then profiled these highly active users and analyzed the type of topics mentioned in their content. More details about the profiling can be seen in our published paper (Flores-Saviaga and Savage 2019).

Our analysis identified three distinct types of users according to behaviors observed. The most interesting type of user was what we called the "pro-Trump trolls." They represented 41.5 percent of the most active users. After analyzing the content, we saw they seemed to employ some of the tactics used by political trolls in the 2016 U.S. political election as they participated in alt-right subreddits such as r/The_Donald. As one of the most active groups identified, these users appeared to be covering and appropriating data voids around Latinxs during the period studied. In this case, as participants covering topics that were more neutral relating to the Latinx community were almost nonexistent, these political trolls were the only ones targeting and covering almost all Latinx-related topics, filling the void.

We detected the introduction of mega-threads to drive numerous people to discuss topics around Latinxs and the midterm elections. Through these mega-threads people on Reddit appeared to contextualize, explain, and discuss in detail the political ecosystem, especially as related to the Latinx community.

Our analysis also uncovered that political trolls created several AMAs (Ask Me Anything sessions) on Reddit with congressional candidates and political personalities where they discussed political topics regarding Latinxs and the midterm elections.

Just as the evidence found in our analysis of The_Donald, during the period before the midterm elections, political trolls appeared to have much more sophisticated techniques for creating engaging content around Latinx and U.S. elections. For example, our research found that political trolls Photoshopped a flyer to include false information about what people should do when stopped by ICE (Silverman 2019).

We call the second group that our research detected the "Latinx Aware anti-Trump." These participants represented 16 percent of the most active users. Posts that the users of this group made referenced the overall migratory situation of Latinxs in the United States, primarily with an emphasis on considering President Trump racist and anti-immigrant. The third group, "The Neutrals," representing 41.5 percent of the most active users, had a more neutral view on the topic of Latinxs and their rights in the United States. This group was, overall, willing to debunk false information being shared on social media regarding Latinxs. However, we found that only 1 percent of their posts were aimed at debunking disinformation.

Therefore, we believed that data voids were being occupied by political trolls, filling them with hateful content and disinformation, while posts from neutral actors were scarcer overall. Thinking strategically about how to engage more neutral actors in the conversation is paramount to limit the existence of data voids being filled with harmful content.

Discussion

Through these data analyses, we uncovered the tactics and behaviors of political trolls during two major political events, the 2016 U.S. presidential election, and the 2018 midterm elections. We believe that, by sharing stories with its community and tweaking them according to their own views, members of The_Donald helped to shift the way people thought about shared information. And this might be one reason why the "Historian" style was one of the most effective strategies for retaining and mobilizing community members. Our results are in alignment with civic technology research. We found that narrating the ideals of what is being fought for (Dimond et al. 2013) and communicating the goals and purpose of the movement (Bennett and Segerberg 2011) help to mobilize members of a community. By tweaking stories according to their own view, The_Donald members framed events in such a way that their opposition (in this case, the "establishment") was somehow discredited. Participating in conspiracy theories was another way to promote their collective identity as it establishes a dynamic in which participants promote stories that the community believes are true and the opposition discredits. Conspiracy theories go back to the 1970s, when the CIA created the term "conspiracy theorist" with the aim of refuting anyone who was against official narratives. Today, the fact that trolls engage in alleged conspiracy theories helps them ensure long-term participation of members of the community because the detailed explanations help individuals to understand the community's reasoning in the current political ecosystem, thus inspiring them to take action.

Analyzing previous studies of online communities, we found that researchers have emphasized the importance of building an identity with community members to facilitate mobilization (Kraut et al. 2012). The unique pro-Trump vocabulary that members of The_Donald used in "Troll Slang" posts was one of the ways in which participants were able to build and grow their own identity. Once a community was strong and solid with a defined identity, it was easier to mobilize large crowds. And this might be one reason why the "Viral News" style, with its very straightforward way of requesting action, was effective at mobilizing large crowds. This matches the findings of online civic platforms research where direct requests usually garnered more participation than the "more manipulative" calls to action (Savage, Monroy-Hernandez, and Höllerer 2016).

Having such direct and simple messages helped individuals save time by not having to read much about the problem being addressed. Additionally, providing users with prefabricated material made them more efficient as they did not have to invest time in creating new material to spread. Instead, they simply focused on executing. In this case, the ability to rapidly take action facilitated participation.

Therefore, "Troll Slang" posts helped to build and grow their own identity, while the "Historian" posts were used to promote the community's belief system (or indoctrinate newcomers). Finally, the "Viral News" posts created opportunities to drive the community to take rapid action when needed without having to explain much in detail about the reasons.

Our research uncovered how—within subversive environments, where the community had large opposition—it was more important to explain the motives of the organization rather than promote an identity for the community. This was essential to rapidly mobilize more people.

Bots within Reddit have been used mainly for automated support for human moderators (Long et al. 2017), upvoting or downvoting posts (Gilbert 2013), and for entertainment (Massanari 2016). However, bots such as TrumpTrainBot used slang that likely also provided the opportunity to promote a sense of identity within The_Donald.

During our analysis of the 2018 midterm elections, once again we saw how these political trolls use the same tactics to target minority groups such as the Latinx community. One realization of our research was that, through the lack of neutral actors engaging Latinxs on political topics, political trolls were able to gain ground. This is problematic because it can cause more neutral members of social groups to pull away from online conversations and platforms. If they decide to stop using them to engage and organize themselves, they further cede ground to trolls and extremists.

As our research on the The_Donald subreddit showed how political trolls used a myriad of tactics to mobilize their participants in political causes, we recommend that mainstream media, politicians, and political organizations adopt some of those strategies for explaining the current political ecosystem to Latinxs. We recommend specifically adopting strategies that will facilitate deep discussions—similar to those used by political trolls. Given that Latinx is the second-largest racial or ethnic group behind whites in the United States, if mobilized they could potentially affect the U.S. elections and create truly better political outcomes for all Latinxs.

We also believe it is important that these institutions take action to actively debunk disinformation regarding Latinxs, such as fake news reports about crimes committed by illegal immigrants, as it appears that only extreme groups are taking advantage of the data voids and filling them with disinformation. We believe that politicians, political organizations, and NGOs have a window of opportunity to facilitate better communication and engagement with the Latinx community.

Limitations

More empirical work needs to be carried out to understand the connections between trolls' individual feelings of belonging, commitment, and identification to a community; how much this results in the community's mobilization; and how the community's collective identity is showcased. The insights this research provides are limited by the methodology and population we studied; as we focused on Reddit, our results might not describe how other similar communities on other social media platforms behave. Additionally, we were unable to uncover the identities of the individual users of Reddit.

REFERENCES

Althoff, T., C. Danescu-Niculescu-Mizil, and D. Jurafsky. 2014. "How to Ask for a Favor: A Case Study on the Success of Altruistic Requests." *Proceedings of the International AAAI Conference on Web and Social Media* 8, no. 1.

Bennett, W. L., and A. Segerberg, A. 2011. "Digital Media and the Personalization of Collective Action: Social Technology and the Organization of Protests against the Global Economic Crisis." *Information, Communication and Society* 14 (6): 770–99.

Bertrand, J. 2016. "It Looks like Russia Hired Internet Trolls to Pose as Pro-Trump Americans." July 27. *Business Insider.* www.businessinsider.com/russia-internet-trolls -and-donald-trump-2016-7.

Bradshaw, S., and P. Howard. 2017. "Troops, Trolls, and Troublemakers: A Global Inventory of Organized Social Media Manipulation." Computational Propaganda Research Project, 2017. University of Oxford.

Cheng, J., C. Danescu-Niculescu-Mizil, J. Leskovec, and M. Bernstein. 2017. "Anyone Can Become a Troll." *American Scientist* 105 (3): 152.

Cheng, J., C. Danescu-Niculescu-Mizil, and J. Leskovec. 2015. "Antisocial Behavior in Online Discussion Communities." *Proceedings of the International AAAI Conference on Web and Social Media* 9, no. 1.

Coles, B. A., and M. West. 2016. "Trolling the Trolls: Online Forum Users' Constructions of the Nature and Properties of Trolling." *Computers in Human Behavior* 60: 233–44.

Crum, M. 2016. "Pro-Trump Trolls Target Megyn Kelly's New Book on Amazon." *Huff-Post.* www.huffpost.com/entry/pro-trump-trolls-target-megyn-kellys-new-book -on-amazon_n_58333eb4e4b099512f840828.

De Choudhury, M., S. Jhaver, B. Sugar, and I. Weber. 2016. "Social Media Participation in an Activist Movement for Racial Equality." *Proceedings of the International AAAI Conference on Web and Social Media* 10, no. 1.

Dimond, J. P., M. Dye, D. LaRose, and A. S. Bruckman. 2013. "Hollaback! The Role of Storytelling Online in a Social Movement Organization." In *Proceedings of the 2013 Conference on Computer Supported Cooperative Work,* 477–90. Association for Computing Machinery.

Ennis, S. 2010. "The Hispanic Population: 2010." U.S. Census Bureau. www.census.gov /prod/cen2010/briefs/c2010br-04.pdf.

Flores-Saviaga, C., B. C. Keegan, and S. Savage. 2018. "Mobilizing the Trump Train: Understanding Collective Action in a Political Trolling Community." June. In 12th International AAAI Conference on Web and Social Media.

Flores-Saviaga C., and S. Savage. 2019. "Anti-Latinx Computational Propaganda in the United States." Institute for the Future.

Gilbert, E. 2013. "Widespread Underprovision on Reddit." In *Proceedings of the 2013 Conference on Computer Supported Cooperative Work*, 803–8. Association for Computing Machinery.

Han, R. 2015. "Defending the Authoritarian Regime Online: China's Voluntary Fifty-Cent Army." *China Quarterly* 224: 1006–25.

Hemphill, L., A. Culotta, and M. Heston. 2013. "Framing in Social Media: How the U.S. Congress Uses Twitter Hashtags to Frame Political Issues." ssrn.com/abstract= 2317335.

Isaac, M. 2020. "Reddit, Acting Against Hate Speech, Bans 'The_Donald' Subreddit." June 29. *New York Times*. nyti.ms/3vGbDBN.

King, G., J. Pan, and M. E. Roberts. 2017. "How the Chinese Government Fabricates Social Media Posts for Strategic Distraction, Not Engaged Argument." *American Political Science Review* 111 (3): 484–501.

Kobb, C. 2017. "People Are Canceling Their Subscriptions to Boycott Netflix's 'Dear White People.'" *Decider.* dcdr.me/2uU85z0.

Kraut, R. E., P. Resnick, S. Kiesler, M. Burke, Y. Chen, N. Kittur, J. Konstan, Y. Ren, and J. Riedl. 2012. *Building Successful Online Communities: Evidence-Based Social Design.* MIT Press.

Krogstad, J. M., M. H. Lopez, G. López, J. S. Passel, and E. Patten. 2016. "Millennials Make Up Almost Half of Latinx Eligible Voters in 2016." January 19. Pew Research Center. pewrsr.ch/2C5q3Qm.

Kumar, S., J. Cheng, and J. Leskovec. 2017. "Antisocial Behavior on the Web: Characterization and Detection." In *Proceedings of the 26th International Conference on World Wide Web Companion*, 947–50. International World Wide Web Conferences Steering Committee.

Kumar, S., J. Cheng, J. Leskovec; and V. Subrahmanian. 2017. "An Army of Me: Sockpuppets in Online Discussion Communities." In *Proceedings of the 26th International Conference on World Wide Web*, 857–66. International World Wide Web Conferences Steering Committee.

Long, K., J. Vines, S. Sutton, P. Brooker, T. Feltwell, B. Kirman, J. Barnett, and S. Lawson. 2017. "'Could You Define That in Bot Terms?' Requesting, Creating, and Using Bots on Reddit." May. In *Proceedings of the 2017 CHI Conference on Human Factors in Computing Systems*, 3488–3500.

Lyons, M. N. 2017. "Ctrl-Alt-Delete: The Origins and Ideology of the Alternative Right." *Political Research Associates.* January 20. politicalresearch.org/2017/01/20/ctrl-alt -delete-report-on-the-alternative-right.

Massanari, A. L. 2016. "Contested Play: The Culture and Politics of Reddit Bots." *Social-bots and Their Friends: Digital Media and the Automation of Sociality,* chap. 6: 110.

Matias, J. N. 2016. "Going Dark: Social Factors in Collective Action against Platform Operators in the Reddit Blackout." In *Proceedings of the 2016 CHI Conference on Human Factors in Computing Systems,* 1138–51. Association for Computing Machinery.

Mills, R. A. 2018. "Pop-Up Political Advocacy Communities on Reddit.com: Sanders-ForPresident and The Donald." *AI and Society* 33 (1): 39–54.

Nelson, L. 2016. "Clinton: I Support Women Registering for the Draft." *Politico.* politi .co/2G4LC3N.

Olson, M. Jr. 2009. *The Logic of Collective Action: Public Goods and the Theory of Groups,* vol. 124. Harvard University Press.

Pater, J. A., Y. Nadji, E. D. Mynatt, and A. S. Bruckman. 2014. "Just Awful Enough: The Functional Dysfunction of the Something Awful Forums." April. In *Proceedings of the SIGCHI Conference on Human Factors in Computing Systems,* 2407–10.

Savage, S., A. Monroy-Hernandez, and T. Höllerer. 2016. "Botivist: Calling Volunteers to Action Using Online Bots." February. In *Proceedings of the 19th ACM Conference on Computer-Supported Cooperative Work and Social Computing,* 813–22.

Schreckinger, B. 2017. "World War Meme." March–April. *Politico.* politi.co/2F5wv98.

Shachaf, P., and N. Hara. 2010. "Beyond Vandalism: Wikipedia Trolls." *Journal of Information Science* 36 (3): 357–70.

Silverman, Craig. 2019. "Extremists Disproportionally Target and Silence Latinos, Muslims, and Jews on Social Media." May 7. *BuzzFeed News.* www.buzzfeednews.com /article/craigsilverman/extremists-disproportionally-target-and-silence-latinos.

Smiley D., B. Medina, and A. Daugherty. 2018. "Nelson, Wasserman Schultz Blocked at Homestead Minor Shelter." June 19. *Miami Herald.* www.miamiherald.com/news /local/community/miami-dade/homestead/article213449739.html.

Summit-Gil, B. 2016. "This Is Why We Can't Have Nice Things: Mapping the Relationship between Online Trolling And Mainstream Culture." Book review. *New Media and Society* 18 (11): 2800–2803. doi.10.1177/1461444816661710.

Thomas, Al. 2017. "Boycott Netflix Is Trending after the Company Teased a New Comedy." *Rare.* rare.us/rare-news/netflix-is-the-subject-of-a-boycott-campaign-after -a-new-comedy-ruffled-feathers-on-the- right/.

Disinformation

A Cybersecurity Perspective

• • •

GOLDEN G. RICHARD III

Disinformation as a Cybersecurity Problem

Disinformation can be damaging on numerous different levels, from challenging the integrity of democratic institutions, such as fair elections (U.S. Senate Select Committee on Intelligence 2019), to slandering specific individuals or corporations (for example, Larkin 2020; Rashid 2019). Disinformation can consist of text, emails, posts to social media, or convincing "deep fake" videos and other media using generative adversarial networks (GANs) (Goodfellow et al. 2014; Tolosana et al. 2020; Kietzmann et al. 2020; Verdoliva 2020). Because of the dense electronic communication network provided by ubiquitous email and access to social media sites such as Twitter and Facebook, news travels fast, and viral disinformation presented as fact can spread quickly without verification. Disinformation campaigns can both be directed and appear to be directed from virtually anywhere. Darknet operators are even offering disinformation as a service, with costs ranging from thousands to hundreds of thousands of dollars, depending on the scope of the campaign (Insikt Group 2019).

Clearly, significant disinformation campaigns have been perpetrated by human actors, frequently with the help of software bots (Briar 2020) that amplify the information by posting content, following other accounts, upvoting, and so forth (Luceri et al. 2019; Ferrara 2020). Studies have shown that at least seventy countries have participated in disinformation campaigns (Alba and Satarino 2019). A thorough discussion of how social bots operate and some mechanisms for detecting them are presented in Ferrara et al. 2016. Rather than rehash these issues, this essay focuses on the enabling technologies poised to make the disinformation problem far worse than it already is, including state-of-the-art malware and botnets, enabled by the appalling state of software and hardware security. In fact, we are creating, maintaining, and expanding a cyber environment which is ripe for disseminating disinformation, supporting attacks against democratic institutions, and fostering attacks against individuals.

The essay also addresses the problems that individuals face when they are targeted by the same advanced cyberattack techniques that can enable widespread propagation of conspiracy theories or political propaganda. Malware can control their electronic devices, act on their behalf, disrupt electronic voting, destroy their reputations or financial standings, produce "evidence" of crimes allegedly committed, and more. That is, malware can not only amplify the disinformation problem but also make citizens unwilling accomplices, and in some cases, direct targets. Modern malware is stealthy, hard to analyze, frequently undetected by personal security products, such as antivirus, and can perform virtually any action that a computer user might perform. Users, even highly technical ones, are ill-equipped to handle these challenges.

The Evolution of Modern Malware

The first self-replicating computer software was postulated by John von Neumann in 1949 and later described in Neumann 1966. Initially, computer viruses were written primarily out of curiosity, as a programming exercise, and later, to establish a persona or reputation. In the 1980s and 1990s, malicious versions appeared, which caused damage by deleting files or making systems inaccessible.

The term "malware" now encompasses many different varieties of malicious software, including viruses, worms, Trojans, backdoors, and more. Generally, viruses replicated "passively," through shared storage media or electronic communication, such as email attachments. Worms intentionally self-replicate, actively targeting and attempting to infect systems. Trojans exhibit some benign and useful behavior with covert, malicious actions mixed in. Backdoors allow remote, unauthorized access to computer systems. Many malware samples exhibit more than one type of replication mechanism and may perform a variety of actions, including stealing personal information, downloading or uploading files, deleting or modifying sensitive data, sending email, activating video or audio devices, and more. Depending on permissions obtained by a malware sample, virtually any action that the computer's owner might perform can also be performed by the malware. In addition to propagation methods and intent, malware can also be differentiated into kernel-level malware and user-level malware. The primary difference is that, while user-level malware operates with the security permissions associated with individual applications or users, kernel-level malware can exercise complete control over the entire operating system—and thus every application that runs on the computer system and all user data. The goals of kernel-level malware are typically to provide backdoor functionality (to allow persistent, unauthorized access and control of a system), and to hide malicious data or processes from scrutiny. An instance of kernel-level malware can employ various techniques to gain access to needed resources and prevent detection, including hooking or modifying system calls, adding new system calls, inserting new kernel modules, and directly patching kernel code. Kernel-level malware is particularly difficult to detect because it can deliberately prevent users and applications from viewing incriminating data or observing malicious processes.

Although there have been advances in exploitation prevention, including Data Execution Prevention (DEP) (Skape and Skywing 2005), non-executable stacks, user-space and kernel-space address randomization (ASLR and KASLR) (Marco-Gisbert and Ripoll 2014), stack canaries, control flow (Abadi et al. 2005) and code-pointer integrity (Kuznetsor et al. 2014), heap-exploitation prevention techniques (Lee et al. 2015), signed kernel drivers, and so forth, attackers are up to the challenge of overriding them. The arms race between offensive and defensive cyber-security is alive and well. Attackers have developed advanced techniques like Return-Oriented Programming (ROP) (Roemer 2012) to overcome defensive measures like data-execution prevention. In response, defenders have formulated strategies to defeat ROP (for example, Onarlioglu et al. 2010; Gupta et al. 2013; the literature in this area is vast, and detailed coverage is beyond the scope of this essay), but that has simply resulted in numerous clever workarounds (for example, Checkoway et al. 2010; Maisuradze, Backes, and Rossow 2016, among many others). Further-more, while defensive techniques are somewhat effective in preventing malware from exploiting software components to gain a foothold in a user's systems, they do little to prevent malware from executing when users inadvertently click on an attachment or install software with co-vert malicious functionality.

The Incentivization of Malware

A radical difference between early malware and modern malware is in-centive. While some of the factors that motivated early virus writers re-main at play, monetization, politicization, and adoption by nation-states have completely changed the landscape (Ruiz 2019). Malware is now used to spread propaganda, target individual users or groups, distrib-ute spam and disinformation, extort ransom, steal banking credentials, target critical infrastructure (Knake 2020), and more (Martindale 2018). While certain types of malware would seem to be out of the scope of a discussion on disinformation, it is imperative to see that the malware ecosystem is increasingly entwined.

Ransomware is the poster child of malware monetization. This type of malware encrypts user files, making them unusable, and extorts ran-som from victims in exchange for decryption keys. Early schemes, like the AIDS Information Introductory Diskette (Bates 1990) were quite primitive and required users to send payment using postal mail to a foreign address (in this case, Panama) in exchange for decryption keys. Current-generation ransomware is much more sophisticated, with payment typically demanded in cryptocurrency. Furthermore, through use of anonymizing network overlays like Tor (Syverson, Dingledine, and Mathewson 2004) and I2P (Zantout et al. 2011), the parties demanding ransom can remain completely anonymous. Many ransomware variants even offer instructions on how to install Tor or I2P and use a chat system running over these anonymizing network overlays to discuss payment in real time. Recently, ransomware authors have discovered new ways of ensuring that victims pay, by exfiltrating user or corporate data, tying the release of this data with nonpayment of ransom.

Malware that mines or steals cryptocurrency (Pastrana and Suarez-Tangil 2019) is also prevalent. One of the most profitable campaigns analyzed among more than 1.2 million malware samples in Pastrana and Suarez-Tangil 2019 mined more than $10 million in Monero cryptocurrency (using the value of Monero as of July 8, 2020, roughly $65 per XMR). Malware authors have also begun to mix cryptocurrency and ransomware campaigns by mining cryptocurrency using the victim's computer resources while awaiting payment. Cryptocurrency-stealing malware is particularly hard to detect, because it accesses files and other data on a computer system in much the same way users might. One ransomware-stealing variant, called CryptoShuffler (U.S. Office of Personnel Management 2019), monitors a user's Windows clipboard and detects when cryptocurrency addresses, such as those used by Bitcoin or Ethereum, are copied and pasted. The malware silently modifies the addresses, changing them into addresses under the attacker's control, causing payments to be diverted to the attacker. Since cryptocurrency transactions are final, the user loses any diverted funds. Detection is extremely difficult as the malicious payload simply interacts with the system clipboard, an operation performed by many benign applications.

The same distribution systems for infecting users with ransomware can facilitate gaining control of their systems, gathering personal information, interacting with social media in unauthorized ways, distributing and reinforcing disinformation, and more. When groups of machines are under the control of a central operator, botnets are formed.

Botnets and Disinformation

Aside from targeting the private data of users, modern malware can also enable botnets, which are large groups of infected computer systems under the control of a malicious actor. Advanced command-and-control systems are used to direct the actions of infected computers, and botnets can be configured to distribute spam email, conduct email "bombing" campaigns, interact with social media, "war dial" to overload phone systems, and more. Because of widespread and persistent Internet connectivity—a phenomenon not present when primitive malware first appeared—large-scale botnets can be quickly assembled and do devastating harm. The creation of these botnets is empowered by widespread vulnerabilities in software and hardware, many of which remain in place for years without security patches being offered. A recent study by Germany's Fraunhofer Institute for Communication (FKIE) (Tung 2020; Weidenbach and vom Dorp 2020) evaluated 127 routers manufactured by seven different companies. Every single router had security vulnerabilities, with many using old software components that have not received security updates in almost a decade. Many of the routers had hard-coded credentials to access the administrative interface of the router that could not be changed. Since routers of this type are deployed in almost every home with Internet access, powerful opportunities for cybercriminals are created. Unfortunately, previous studies mirror these results, and numerous other hardware and software vulnerabilities open additional avenues for exploitation. Finally, in addition to software and hardware exploitation tactics, botnets are frequently constructed and expanded using social engineering tactics, by tricking users into clicking on attachments in email or visiting malicious websites.

The notorious banking Trojan called Emotet, which emerged in 2014, is frequently spread via infected document files attached to emails. These documents are purported to be invoices, information about package deliveries, and so forth. When a malicious document is opened, it silently downloads additional software components from a command-and-control server. The command-and-control servers also allow the malware authors to update the malware in place on a user's system, to add new functions, exfiltrate user data, and more. Emotet has been significantly expanded since its introduction and is now used to deliver additional malware and distribute spam. In addition to spreading through malicious documents, it has other propagation methods, including brute-forcing passwords to other systems on the local network and using contacts discovered on an infected machine to send targeted emails. By maliciously injecting responses into legitimate email threads copied from infected machines, Emotet is able to trick users into opening infected attachments (Nagy 2019). Newer variations attempt to connect to wireless networks associated with an infected machine, targeting other computers on those networks (O'Donnell 2020). Emotet has now grown into a large botnet, organized into multiple tiers which apparently do not communicate with each other. Recently, the actors behind Emotet launched a disinformation campaign targeting Japanese users by sending emails purportedly from a disability service provider in Japan. These emails contain illegitimate reports about COVID-19 infections and urge users to open attached malicious documents, resulting in malware infection (Seals 2020).

The widespread deployment of Internet of Things (IoT) devices, many of which are plagued with security issues, has made creation of extremely large botnets even easier. The most famous IoT bot, Mirai (Herzberg, Bekerman, and Zeifman 2016), was estimated to have infected between 800,000 and 2.5 million devices (Laliberte 2018). Because the source code for Mirai was leaked, numerous variants based on this malware strain have been released, including Satori, Okiru, Masuta, PureMasuta, OMG, Jenx, Wicked Mirai, covid (Voolf and Cohen 2020), and many more.

Linux/Moose, a botnet that infected routers running Linux, spread rapidly by brute-forcing credentials and actively destroying other resident malware (Bilodeaux and Dupuy 2015). Linux/Moose stole HTTP cookies from social media sites visited by victims, allowing it to issue unauthorized follows, likes, and page views on Facebook, Instagram, YouTube, Twitter, and other sites. Even without posting messages, the activities of bots like these can be used to dramatically alter the metrics that users rely on to judge public support for particular individuals, points of view, or activities.

Malware, Disinformation, and Voting Systems
Dangers to Voting Systems

We now turn to the interplay between disinformation, malicious actors, malware, and voting. This is particularly important in light of recent concerns about in-person voting raised by the 2020 COVID crisis. But despite a vast amount of literature pointing out vulnerabilities of electronic voting systems (Dunn and Merkle 2018; Park et al. 2021; Blaze et al. 2017; Blaze et al. 2018), states in the United States continue to expand electronic voting and some are considering using online voting systems, which allow voters to cast a ballot from a computer or mobile device (Geller 2020). Internet-based voting is dramatically more insecure than electronic voting systems that require a voter to visit a polling station. Many of these reasons are outlined in recent letters to the Cybersecurity and Infrastructure Security Agency (CISA) (Greenhalgh et al. 2020) and to governors and secretaries of state (AAAS 2020), authored by prominent cybersecurity experts. Online voting offers a vast number of targets to exploit, and experts are nearly unanimous in believing that we will have no viable, secure methods for online voting in the near future (Jefferson 2020). Furthermore, as discussed in Jefferson 2020, there is a tendency to equate the widespread adoption of "secure" online commerce with the potential for "secure" online voting. Arguments of this variety miss many significant differences.

First, the motivation to tamper with voting on a large scale is much stronger. Second, the security and privacy requirements for the two activities are quite different. According to pymnts.com, ecommerce fraud reached 3.85 percent in the second quarter of 2017, resulting in over $57 billion in losses across eight industries. Fraud for higher-valued purchases, that is, those exceeding $500, was 11.65 percent. These losses are "silently" borne by the affected ecommerce sites. There is simply no room for this amount of error in political elections. Furthermore, no mechanisms to recoup or redistribute losses is available. Unlike ecommerce transactions, which record the specific account associated with a purchase, only individual voters know which candidate they chose, and there is no way to associate a voter with a particular vote after the vote is cast. The latest buzzword in electronic voting is using blockchain technologies. Prominent cybersecurity experts point out that these efforts, too, are misguided (Park et al. 2021).

Clearly, the malicious techniques already discussed offer numerous methods to corrupt the voting process. Online authentication of voters is problematic since schemes to validate voters based on knowledge of date of birth, Social Security numbers, and so forth, are compromised by vast data leaks that make this information readily available to attackers. Such leaks include information about 150 million Adobe customers in 2013; 450 million customers for Adult Friend Finder in 2016, with poor password storage resulting in compromise of all account data; 145 million eBay users in 2014, including usernames, addresses, dates of birth, and more; 148 million consumers during the Equifax breach of 2017, revealing Social Security numbers, birth dates, addresses, drivers' license numbers; a staggering 3 billion user accounts in Yahoo's breach in 2013–14, with names, email addresses, birth dates, telephone numbers, and more leaked (Swinhoe 2020); and 800 gigabytes of data affecting 200 million U.S. individuals leaked from an unknown source (but suspected to be the U.S. Census), containing full names, email addresses, phone numbers, birth dates, credit ratings, home addresses, demographic information, mortgage and tax records, and more (Spadafora 2020). In 2015, the U.S. Office of Personnel Management (OPM) was breached, revealing highly sensitive information related to security clearances of more than 20 million individuals (U.S. Office of Personnel Management

2019). Unfortunately, this list is far from exhaustive, with a Wikipedia (2020) page tracking roughly three hundred breaches like this since 2014. The real list is likely far longer.

Online voting provides attackers with the opportunity to perform distributed denial-of-service attacks (DDOS), overwhelming servers that collect votes and potentially preventing groups of voters from casting their votes. These servers are also ripe targets for exploitation, to modify or delete votes that have been cast. Any confidence that the systems can be secured is undermined by casual reflection on the data breaches discussed above.

Even hybrid systems, which provide only downloadable ballots, are susceptible to attack. An electronically marked ballot exposes the user not only to data leakage, where information about the vote may persist and be recoverable by malware or memory forensics techniques, but to tampering as well. Malware infecting the document viewer (for example, Adobe Acrobat or Preview) can present an invalid ballot, with choices that differ from those on the official ballot, with the choices reordered, or some other mechanism to ultimately cause the ballot to be rejected. Electronically submitting the document is also fraught with user side risks, as the document viewer may present content different from what is stored in the PDF file. Even printing the document may be insufficient, as print functions in the document viewer could be similarly compromised. Aside from checking the electronic ballot using a dedicated system that has been isolated to prevent infection, the user might still submit a ballot reflecting someone else's choices. Even downloading, printing, and then physically marking up an electronic ballot is subject to interference, as malware can intercept the ballot in the user's web browser and apply the same measures to cause the ballot to be ultimately rejected and the vote lost.

The preferable method for conducting an election where individuals cannot visit a polling station, such as it might be under the COVID-19 crisis, is reception of a paper ballot in the mail, to be marked by hand and then returned via postal mail.

Disinformation and the Trojan Defense

Disinformation is not a strictly global phenomenon. Malicious actors and malware can target individuals or groups and plant false information intended to cause embarrassment, loss of reputation or employment, or civil or criminal liability. Because of the complexity and stealth exhibited by modern attackers and malware, separating the actions performed by a user from those performed by a malicious actor can be exceedingly difficult. State-of-the-art malware can surreptitiously perform any action a computer user can perform, including sending emails, surfing websites, downloading files and categorizing them, executing attacks against other computer systems, and more. Often, all owners can reasonably do is plead their innocence.

The Trojan defense, also known as the "some other dude did it" (SODDI) defense, is likely the oldest legal defense. This tactic asserts that the accused is innocent and that some other party is responsible. Since the advent of malware, this defense also includes nonhuman entities, like computer software. The SODDI defense is traditionally met with skepticism, often well-deserved, but in many cases the accused person's livelihood and life may depend on an accurate assessment of the facts. Unfortunately, a relatively standard procedure for refuting the Trojan defense in cases where malware is blamed is to perform a forensics investigation and run an antivirus product on the accused's computer system(s). Lack of detection is then essentially a "refutation" of the defense.

The strategy of relying on traditional digital investigative techniques, combined with antivirus scans, mirrors strategies discussed in "The Trojan Horse Defense in Cybercrime Cases" (Brenner, Carrier, and Henn 2004), written more than fifteen years ago. That paper suggests a two-pronged approach for prosecutors to refute the SODDI, specifically, that investigators "establish the defendant's computer expertise" and "negate the factual foundation of the defense." The former goal is based on experiences those authors had with defendants using the SODDI also claiming to have little computer expertise, essentially making them particularly vulnerable to malware or an attacker. While it is reasonable to assume that someone accused of a crime would attempt to make their SODDI claim as plausible as possible by introducing the issue of technical aptitude, it is arguable that, to some degree, aptitude is a red herring. Not only can modern malware evade detection by antivirus, but even technical users have significant difficulty in establishing the legitimacy of websites and differentiating phishing emails from legitimate ones. Recent studies continue to illustrate that users aren't very good at detecting phishing attacks (Iuga, Nurse, and Erola 2016) and that technical expertise is not correlated with better detection (Alsharnouby, Alaca, and Chaisson 2015). Alarmingly, some studies reveal "educated users and those with high levels of privacy concerns being most susceptible to harm" (Blank and Lutz 2018).

The second prong is to conduct an intensive digital forensics investigation. Typical steps taken in such an investigation are discussed in Section Digital Forensics. But as we'll see there, traditional digital forensics techniques are not sufficient for investigating many strains of modern malware, which may be memory-only, fileless, and leave virtually no traces on storage devices. If the investigative effort is truly carried out with all of the technical tools available to us today, including memory forensics (discussed in Section Memory Forensics, below), then the chances of detecting and analyzing malware (or refuting a SODDI claim) is increased, but this not only requires advanced technical skills (which are in short supply), but is also expensive.

Steel (2014) discusses numerous SODDI cases in detail. The author points out that, while SODDI defenses are often successful in civil cases, he was aware of no successful acquittals in the criminal domain. Most of the criminal cases discussed involved child pornography, and other compelling evidence was frequently available.

Details of a private case in which the author was involved are presented next, to illustrate some of the technical issues that SODDI defenses may present. The case involved the termination of a female employee who was accused of accessing NSFW materials at work—specifically, visiting and retrieving images from online pornographic sites. The employee claimed innocence, but network logs created by the company's

IT staff clearly showed access to these sites from the employee's computer, and furthermore, only when she was in her office. A preliminary forensic examination of her system revealed dozens of pornographic images in the Internet Explorer browser cache and numerous entries in web history, all indicating intentional access to the pornographic sites.

More detailed analysis of the computer, performed when the employee continued to insist that she was innocent, revealed malware was present. Prior antivirus scans had failed to detect the malware, and it was detected solely because of its use of a very common mechanism for persistence (that is, manipulation of a RUN key in the Windows registry, which governs which applications start automatically when the machine is rebooted). The use of this relatively easy-to-detect persistence mechanism was curious and a stroke of luck for the employee, as the malware itself was sophisticated (and extremely difficult to analyze manually). It communicated with a remote server to drop additional malicious components on the victim's system and then manipulated Internet Explorer to surf various pornographic sites without presenting the usual graphical interface by directly accessing functions in the ShDocVw.dll dynamic library (a component of Internet Explorer). The surfing activity was triggered by use of the affected system's keyboard, ensuring the party using the computer would be held liable for accessing the sites. Absolutely no visual signs of the web-surfing activities were apparent to the user of the computer system. By controlling Internet Explorer directly, the web history and cache files were populated precisely as if the user had deliberately accessed the sites.

An important question is whether the malware would have been detected if the persistence mechanism had not given it away. When the malware sample was analyzed using thirty-one different antivirus products, twenty of them tagged it as benign, including ClamAV, F-Prot, Kaspersky, McAfee, and Microsoft's products. Eleven of the products flagged the file as malware, but in every instance, the file was determined simply to be "generic" malware, meaning that it exhibits suspicious behavior, but no details or clues for further investigation of the malicious behavior were provided.

The intention of Brenner, Carrier, and Henninger 2004 is not to strip the accused of their potentially only line of defense, but rather to counter spurious use of the SODDI: "Our goal, then, is to explain how to negate the defense when it is simply a 'defense tactic': a technologically-based SODDI defense. It is not our intention to discredit the Trojan horse defense, as there will no doubt be instances in which its invocation will be well-founded. Therefore, we seek only to explain how it can be negated when it is being used in an attempt to prevent the conviction of someone who is demonstrably guilty."

The point of the current discussion is similarly not to suggest we throw up our hands in despair and say we simply cannot rely on electronic evidence. Rather, it is to call attention to the fact that traditional and relatively simplistic digital forensics investigations will typically not be effective in unwinding deliberate disinformation campaigns involving sophisticated malware or attackers. Furthermore, computers are not only increasingly involved in crimes, but in many cases provide the only evidence that a crime has been committed. Given the capabilities exhibited by modern malware, the extremely difficult task of detecting and analyzing it, and the costs involved in performing such analysis, we should at the very least be more receptive to the possibility that a SODDI defense is valid, especially in situations where the accused faces life-altering (or life-ending) punishment.

User Awareness and Perception

Given these threats, how do computer users perceive the threats, and what defensive tactics might they employ? While better user education concerning the threats they face online may help, there are currently few technical solutions available to protect users from advanced malware. Users are often told to run antivirus software and, while these products work to some degree, they are most effective against well-known and previously analyzed threats. Users are also instructed to obey the usual "cyber-hygiene" rules, including changing default passwords and not reusing passwords, not clicking on unknown email attachments, not visiting unknown websites, and keeping operating systems and applications up-to-date. In many cases, users do not correctly perceive what threats are even possible, much less pay adequate attention to them. In numerous studies, user inattention or ambivalence to security issues has been established (Felt et al. 2012; Eargle, Galletta, and Jenkins 2016; Hwang et al. 2017).

Despite the very serious concerns about online voting, an alarming 49 percent of users in a recent poll (TargetSmart 2020) indicated their support for voting over the Internet in U.S. elections. This is despite prominent experts warning the U.S. government against Internet voting and pointing out woefully inadequate security measures in U.S. Cybersecurity and Infrastructure Security Agency report (Greenhalgh et al. 2020). It is therefore very likely that users on the front line, who encounter new zero-day threats, will be affected. In fact, experts question whether it is even reasonable for users to be expected to manage their own cybersecurity concerns (Prenaud et al. 2018), given that the technical considerations are beyond most users' capabilities and very little concrete assistance is available. Exacerbating this problem is that users often need not explicitly perform any risky actions at all, other than simply purchasing a hardware device or installing an application. This is because many hardware and software components are vulnerable out of the box. Simply deploying these components exposes users to substantial hidden risks.

Many computer users apparently maintain, either consciously or unconsciously, a "cyber world view" in almost direct contradiction to models like Descartes's imaginary demon (Descartes 2013), described as having "utmost power and cunning" and having "employed all his energies in order to deceive me." This is likely a result of two factors. First, for the types of threat individual users are aware of, they may imagine they are taking whatever precautions they can. But it is conceivable that most users can scarcely imagine the breadth and depth of cyberattacks that are possible today. Second, cyberattacks are contagious. Regardless of whether users have attempted to take precautions and are compromised or if they are willfully oblivious, infected computers affect a much broader population than the owner of one computer, since they can be used to compromise privileged multi-party communications, as a vector for creating botnets for widespread attacks, or dissemination of disinformation and more. This is in sharp contrast to threats like fire, for example, which are more localized and for which more resources are made available to potential victims by government institutions (Prenaud et al. 2018).

Technical Solutions

There are promising technical solutions to combat malware and disinformation, but for the most part they are not yet suitable for deployment on end-user systems. Most are investigative and useful to determine the nature of an attack that has already occurred and possibly to identify the attackers. We will examine some technical solutions to discovering and analyzing malware that might be used in disinformation campaigns, whether against the general public or specific individuals. While complete solutions are unavailable, digital forensics and memory forensics play a significant role in combating disinformation and protecting users.

Digital Forensics

Traditionally, digital forensics techniques are used to preserve and analyze digital evidence stored on computer systems, cell phones, and other digital devices. These digital forensics techniques target nonvolatile storage devices, such as hard drives. The typical workflow is to power down a target machine, make exact copies of its storage devices, and employ a variety of techniques to recover evidence. These techniques include data carving (Richard and Roussev 2005) to retrieve deleted data, generation of timelines to determine affected files (Buchholz and Falk 2005; Inglot, Liu, and Antonopoulos 2012), and analysis of the Windows registry (Carvey, Harrell, and Shavers 2012; Carvey 2011). A major issue is determining if malware is present and, if it is, extracting a sample of the malware for reverse engineering to see where it came from and what it does.

Data-carving techniques use databases of headers and footers, which are strings of bytes at predictable offsets in a file, or more complete file specifications, to identify the start and end locations of files or other data to recreate deleted files. A common method to infect systems is to spread malicious executables which then download additional components during the infection process, possibly deleting some of these components. This makes file carving an important strategy in recovering deleted executables for analysis. One limitation of the current generation of data-carving tools is that the data must generally be stored contiguously on the storage device to be fully recoverable. This is usually not a serious problem on modern systems, however, as malware executables tend to be small and modern computers have abundant storage.

Generating forensic timelines is useful in several ways. First, when investigating malware infections, it allows an investigator to establish when specific files were created, accessed, and modified. Timelining also allows pinpointing the specific times when media were created, which could include the source materials and final product in the generation of deep fakes.

Analysis of system configuration data, such as the Windows registry, can help investigators discover malware as well as establish whether certain malware persistence techniques were employed. It was the use of a common persistence technique that upheld a SODDI defense involving access to illicit websites while an employee was at work. These persistence techniques often use the Windows registry to ensure that the malware sample will execute each time the system is restarted. More stealthy persistence mechanisms are in wide use (MITRE Corporation 2019), and some are trickier to detect.

Other digital forensics techniques are also common, including the examination of web-browser history and caches, to shed light on surfing activities. Network and application logs are also scrutinized to determine when users logged in, whether network-scanning activities have been employed, whether applications crashed because of tampering by malware, and so on. For many civil as well as criminal cases, especially when supporting physical evidence is available, these traditional digital forensics techniques perform well and are sufficiently powerful to reveal both incriminating and exculpatory evidence. When sophisticated malware is involved, however, these techniques fall well short. Modern malware may be file-less or in-memory only (Skape and Turkulainen 2004; Volexity 2016; Bencsáth et al. 2011; Kaspersky Lab 2014; Dell Secureworks 2015), meaning that it may leave absolutely no traces on a computer system's storage devices. This may result in signs of malware infection being completely missed, particularly if the machine is powered down to make copies of storage devices, which is typical. Supplementing these techniques to address detection of modern malware is essential, and memory forensics offers great promise.

Memory Forensics

Over the last fifteen years, memory forensics (Ligh et al. 2014; Ali-Gombe, Case, and Richard 2019; Song et al. 2018; Saltaformaggio et al. 2016; Case and Richard 2015; Case and Richard 2014; Sylve et al. 2012; Case et al. 2010; Case, Marziale, and Richard 2010; Richard 2010; Richard and Ahmed 2014; Ahmed and Richard 2014) has supplemented digital forensics techniques, offering a better idea of what has occurred and what is happening on a computer system. Memory forensics techniques analyze a snapshot of a system's volatile storage (RAM) instead of concentrating solely on data stored on nonvolatile storage devices. Since almost any operation on a computer system induces changes in RAM, memory forensics can offer a much more complete picture than traditional digital forensics techniques. The evidence recoverable through memory forensics includes lists of processes that have executed on the computer system, active and closed network connections, memory-only malware code, hooks inserted by malware to influence system behaviors, and more.

One problem with many malware-detection techniques is that they require a particular malware sample to have been previously analyzed. The appearance of targeted malware, designed explicitly for an attack against an individual, a corporation, or a nation-state, requires techniques able to detect all malware and not only malware belonging to previously analyzed families. The author and his collaborators are working on various memory forensics techniques designed to discover whenever malware is present on a system and provide deeper analysis capabilities, regardless of whether the malware has been seen before.

In memory forensics research funded by the National Science Foundation, the author, along with Andrew Case, Aisha Ali-Gombe, and a host of students, are working on problems in memory forensics. First, we are creating a large and diverse collection of freely available, realistic datasets for memory forensics research and practice. One issue with current memory forensics techniques is that they recover so many artifacts that investigators are easily overwhelmed. To deal with this situation, investigators will frequently start by investigating a "known good" system, running the same operating system and application versions as a targeted system, to understand the system's "normal" state. Once "normal" is understood, anomalous artifacts can quickly be filtered out. Our well-documented set of memory images offers "ground truth" and presents a solution to this problem.

Our research effort also includes the creation of tools to automate the tedious and error-prone process of ensuring that memory forensics toolsets operate correctly and produce accurate results. Memory forensics frameworks consist of complex code bases. For every artifact an analysis tool recovers from a memory sample, it must typically re-implement one or more algorithms used by an operating system or application. Furthermore, tools must also perfectly replicate the layout of data structures processed by these algorithms to produce correct results. Generating incorrect results (or no results at all) due to coding errors can lead to dire consequences, allowing dangerous malware to go undetected. This is particularly problematic as memory forensics becomes more automated, with no human investigator evaluating each step. Our solution was to develop a massively parallel fuzzing platform for memory forensics tools, called Gaslight (Case et al. 2017; Shahmirza 2019; Paruchuri, Case, and Richard 2020), which intelligently modifies memory images to simulate both acquisition errors as well as malicious tampering. Gaslight stress tests memory forensics tools to find errors in the implementations, which are flagged for correction by the developers of the tools. This is necessary to ensure that memory forensics frameworks provide accurate results.

We are also expanding the scope of memory forensics to better detect and analyze userland malware (Case et al. 2020). We have created tools to discover and analyze advanced malware affecting Mac operating systems (Case and Richard 2016) as well as techniques to forensically analyze the Windows Subsystem for Linux (WSL) (Lewis et al. 2018). WSL essentially provides a complete Linux runtime environment inside of Windows 10. Prior to this work, there were no memory forensics tools for analyzing malware that might utilize WSL. We have also conducted pioneering research in the use of emulation in detecting and generating descriptive indicators of compromise for userland malware, based solely on memory images of infected machines (Case et al. 2019; Case et al. 2020). This system is called HookTracer and offers a valuable resource in detecting memory-only and file-less malware, including state-of-the-art keystroke loggers and other malware that hooks operating system and application functions. Finally, we are currently developing new detection and analysis capabilities for malware that has a direct, negative impact on targeted individuals and organizations, motivated by a rash of incidents of this kind (Prince 2014; Kaspersky 2014b; Reuters 2019; Gatlan 2019; Scott-Railton et al. 2017; Marczak et al. 2016; Brooks et al. 2016; Kaspersky 2014a). This research involves development of deep memory forensics techniques to investigate compromises of web and database servers. It is our conviction that memory forensics plays a crucial role in battling modern malware and making systems safer.

We acknowledge that a persistent problem with digital forensics and memory forensics techniques is that the investigative procedures are still mostly reactive and require substantial amounts of manual investigative effort, typically performed by an experienced investigator. We are hopeful that our work will ultimately support more autonomous and automated solutions to automatically detect and remediate malicious software of all kinds, including malware that supports disinformation campaigns.

This work was supported in part by the National Science Foundation through grant no. 1703683. I am very grateful to Elsa Hahne for offering a great deal of helpful feedback on drafts of this essay. I would also like to acknowledge my many collaborators for helpful discussions, and in particular, Andrew Case, a leading memory forensics researcher and incident response expert.

REFERENCES

AAAS [American Association for the Advancement of Science]. 2020. "Letter to Governors and Secretaries of State on the Insecurity of Online Voting." April 9. www.aaas .org/programs/epi-center/internet-voting-letter.

Abadi, M., M. Budiu, U. Erlingsson, and J. Ligatti. 2005. "CFI: Principles, Implementations, and Applications." In *Proc. ACM Conference and Computer and Communications Security (CCS)*.

Ahmed, I., and G. G. Richard III. 2014. "Kernel Pool Monitoring for Live Forensics." In *Proceedings of the 66th Annual Meeting of the American Academy of Forensic Sciences (AAFS)*.

Alba, D., and A. Satariano. 2019. "At Least 70 Countries Have Had Disinformation Campaigns, Study Finds." September 26. *New York Times.* www.nytimes.com/2019 /09/26/technology/government-disinformation-cyber-troops.html.

Ali-Gombe, A., A. Case, and G. G. Richard III. 2019. "DroidScraper: A Tool for Android In-Memory Object Recovery and Reconstruction." In *22nd International Symposium on Research in Attacks, Intrusions and Defenses (RAID 2019)*, 547–59.

Alsharnouby, M., F. Alaca, and S. Chaisson. 2015. "Why Phishing Still Works: User Strategies for Combatting Phishing Attacks." *International Journal of Human-Computer Studies* 82: 69–82.

Bates, J. 1990. "Trojan Horse: AIDS Information Introductory Diskette Version 2.0." *Virus Bulletin,* 3–6.

Bencsáth, B., G. Pek, L. Buttyan, and M. Felegyhazi. 2011. "Duqu: A Stuznet-like Malware Found in the Wild." October 14. *CrySyS Lab, Technical Report* 14.

Bilodeau, O., and T. Dupuy. 2015. "Dissecting Linux/Moose." www.welivesecurity.com /wp-content/uploads/2015/05/Dissecting-LinuxMoose.pdf.

Blank, G., and C. Lutz. 2018. "Benefits and Harms from Internet Use: A Differentiated Analysis of Great Britain." *New Media and Society* 20 (2): 618–40.

Blaze, M., J. Braun, and Cambridge Global Advisors. 2017. "DEFCON 25 Voting Machine Hacking Village." *Proceedings of DEFCON.* Washington, DC, 1–18.

Blaze, M., J. Braun, H. Hursti, D. Jefferson, M. MacAlpine, and J. Moss. 2018. "DEFCON 26 Voting Village: Report on Cyber Vulnerabilities in U.S. Election Equipment, Databases, and Infrastructure." *DEFCON* 26.

Brenner, S. W., B. Carrier, and J. Henninger. 2004. "The Trojan Horse Defense in Cybercrime Cases." *Santa Clara Computer and High Tech. Law Journal* 21 (1).

Briar, J. 2020. "Disinformation in 5.4 Billion Fake Accounts: A Lesson for the Private Sector." *Security Magazine*. www.securitymagazine.com/articles/91616-disinformation-in-54-billion-fake-accounts-a-lesson-for-the-private-sector.

Brooks, M., J. Dalek, and M. Crete-Nishihata. 2016. "Between Hong Kong and Burma: Tracking UP007 and SLServer Espionage Campaigns." April 18. *TheCitizenLab*. citizenlab.ca/2016/04/between-hong-kong-and-burma/.

Buchholtz, F. P., and C. Falk. 2005. "Design and Implementation of Zeitline: A Forensic Timeline Editor." In *Proceedings of the Digital Forensics Research Conference*.

Roemer, R., E. Buchanan, H. Shacham, and S. Savage. 2012. "Return-Oriented Programming: Systems, Languages, and Applications." ACM Transactions on Information and System Security (TISSEC) 15, no. 1 (2012): 1–34.

Carvey, H. 2011. *Windows Registry Forensics: Advanced Digital Forensic Analysis of the Windows Registry*. Elsevier.

———, C. Harrell, and B. Shavers. 2012. "RegRipper." github.com/keydet89/RegRipper3.0.

Case, A., A. Ali-Gombe, M. Sun, R. Maggio, M. Firoz-Ul-Amin, M. Jalalai, and G. G. Richard III. 2019. "HookTracer: A System for Automated and Accessible API Hooks Analysis." *Proceedings of the 18th Annual Digital Forensics Research Conference (DFRWS)*.

Case, A., A. Das, S. Park, R. Ramanujam, and G. G. Richard III. 2017. "Gaslight: A Comprehensive Fuzzing Architecture for Memory Forensics Frameworks." *Proceedings of the 2017 Digital Forensics Research Conference (DFRWS)*.

Case, A., R. Maggio, M. Firoz-Ul-Amin, M. Jalazai, A. Ali-Gombe, M. Sun, and G. G. Richard III. 2020. "Hooktracer: Automatic Detection and Analysis of Keystroke Loggers Using Memory Forensics." *Computers and Security* 96.

Case, A., R. Maggio, M. Manna, and G. G. Richard III. 2020. "Memory Analysis of macOS Page Queues." *Digital Forensics Research Conference (DFRWS)*.

Case, A., L. Marziale, C. Neckar, and G. G. Richard III. 2010. "Treasure and Tragedy in kmem_cache Mining for Live Forensics Investigation." *Proceedings of the 10th Annual Digital Forensics Research Workshop (DFRWS)*.

Case, A., L. Marziale, and G. G. Richard III. 2010. "Dynamic Recreation of Kernel Data Structures for Live Forensics." *Proceedings of the 10th Annual Digital Forensics Research Workshop (DFRWS)*.

Case, A., and G. G. Richard III. 2014. "In Lieu of Swap: Analyzing Compressed RAM in Mac OS X and Linux." *Proceedings of the 14th Annual Digital Forensics Research Workshop (DFRWS)*.

———. 2015. "Advancing Mac OS X Rootkit Detection." *Proceedings of the 15th Annual Digital Forensics Research Workshop (DFRWS)*.

———. 2016. "Detecting Objective-C Malware through Memory Forensics." *Proceedings of the 16th Annual Digital Forensics Research Workshop (DFRWS).*

Checkoway, S., L. Davi, A. Dmitrienko, A. Sadeghi, H. Shacham, and M. Winandy. 2010. "Return-Oriented Programming without Returns." In *Proceedings of the 17th ACM Conference on Computer and Communications Security,* 559–72.

Dell SecureWorks Counter Threat Unit Threat Intelligence 2015. "Skeleton Key Malware Analysis." January 12. *Secureworks.* www.secureworks.com/research/skeleton -key-malware-analysis.

Descartes, R. 2013. [First published in Latin in 1641.] *Rene Descartes: Meditations on First Philosophy.* Cambridge University Press.

Dunn, M., and L. Merkle. 2018. "Overview of Software Security Issues in Direct-Recording Electronic Voting Machines." In *ICCWS 2018 13th International Conference on Cyber Warfare and Security.* Academic Conferences and Publishing Ltd.

Eargle, D., D. F. Galletta, and J. L. Jenkins. 2016. "What's It Worth to You? Applying Risk Tradeoff Paradigms to Explain User Interactions with Interruptive Security Messages." *Proceedings of the Workshop on Information Security and Privacy.*

Felt, A., E. Ha, S. Egelman, and D. Wagner. 2012. "Android Permissions: User Attention, Comprehensive, and Behavior." In *Proceedings of the Eighth Symposium on Usable Privacy and Security,* 1–14.

Ferrera, E. 2020. "Bots, Elections, and Social Media: A Brief Overview." In *Disinformation, Misinformation, and Fake News in Social Media,* ed. K. Shu et al. Springer. 95–114.

———, O. Varol, C. Davis, F. Menczer, and A. Flamminni. 2016. "The Rise of Social Bots." *Communications of the ACM* 59 (7): 96–107.

Gatlan, S. 2019. "New Malware Spies on Diplomats, High-Profile Government Targets." October 10. *BleepingComputer.* www.bleepingcomputer.com/news/security/new -malware-spies-on-diplomats-high-profile-government-targets/.

Geller, E. 2020. "Some States Have Embraced Online Voting. It's a Huge Risk." June 8. *Politico.* www.politico.com/news/2020/06/08/online-voting-304013.

Goodfellow, I., J. Pouget-Abaie, M. Mirza, B. Xu, D. Warde-Farley, S. Ozar, A. Courville, and Y. Bengio. 2014. "Generative Adversarial Nets." In *Advances in Neural Information Processing Systems,* 2672–80.

Greenhalgh, S., et al. 2020. Letter to CISA. context-cdn.washingtonpost.com/notes /prod/default/documents/4ac156b8-9f4d-4df1-95d8-2be023c2559c/note/ba1499e1 -4f98-4b96-9dbf-afe99d96e6e0.

Gupta, A., S. Kerr, M. S. Kirkpatrick, and E. Bertino. 2013. "Marlin: A Fine Grained Randomization Approach to Defend Against ROP Attacks." *In International Conference on Network and System Security.* Springer. 293–306.

Herzberg, B., D. Bekerman, and I. Zeifman. 2016. "Breaking Down Mirai: An IoT DDoS Botnet Analysis." www.imperva.com/blog/malware-analysis-mirai-ddos-botnet/.

Hwang, I., D. Kim, T. Kim, and S. Kim. 2017. "Why Not Comply with Information Security? An Empirical Approach for the Causes of Non-compliance." *Online Information Review.*

Inglot B., L. Liu, and N. Antonopoulos. 2012. "A Framework for Enhanced Timeline Analysis in Digital Forensics." In *2012 IEE International Conference on Green Computing and Communications.* IEEE. 253–56.

Insikt Group. 2019. "The Price of Influence: Disinformation in the Private Sector." September 30. *Recorded Future.* www.recordedfuture.com/disinformation-service-campaigns/.

Iuga, C., J. Nurse, and A. Erola. 2016. "Baiting the Hook: Factors Impacting Susceptibility to Phishing Attacks." *Human-centric Computing and Information Sciences* 6 (1).

Jefferson, D. (2020). "If I Can Shop and Bank Online, Why Can't I Vote Online?—Verified Voting." *Verified Voting.* verifiedvoting.org/publication/if-i-can-shop-and-bank-online-why-cant-i-vote-online/.

Kaspersky. 2014a. "The Syrian Malware House of Cards." August 18. *Securelist by Kaspersky.* securelist.com/the-syrian-malware-house-of-cards/66051/.

Kaspersky. 2014b. "The Darkhotel APT." November 10. *Securelist by Kaspersky.* securelist.com/the-syrian-malware-house-of-cars/66051/.

Kaspersky Lab. 2014. "Kaspersky Lab Uncovers 'The Mask': One of the Most Advanced Global Cyber-espionage Operations to Date Due to the Complexity of the Toolset Used by Attackers." February 10. *Kaspersky.* usa.kaspersky.com/about/press-releases/2014_kaspersky-lab-uncovers--the-mask--one-of-the-most-advanced-global-cyber-espionage-operations-to-date-due-to-the-complexity-of-the-toolset-used-by-the-attackers.

Kietzmann, J., L. W. Lee, I. P. McCarthy, and T. C. Kietzmann. (2020). "Deepfakes: Trick or Treat?" *Business Horizons* 63 (2): 135–46.

Knake, R. 2020. "Top Conflicts to Watch in 2020: A Cyberattack on U.S. Critical Infrastructure." Council on Foreign Relations. www.cfr.org/blog/top-conflicts-watch-2020-cyberattack-us-critical-infrastructure.

Kuznetsov, V., L. Szekeres, M. Payer, G. Candea, R. Sekar, and D. Song. 2014. "Code-pointer Integrity." In *10th USENIX Symposium on Operating Systems Design and Implementation (OSDI).*

Laliberte, M. 2018. "IoT Botnets are Evolving—How Big Can They Get?" February 20. *Secplicity.* www.secplicity.org/2018/02/20/iot-botnets-evolving-big-can-get/.

Larkin, X. 2020. "You Can't Just Get Up and Steal a Police Horse." July 1. *New York Times.* www.nytimes.com/2020/07/01/style/dreadhead-cowboy-chicago.html.

Lee, B., C. Song, Y. Jang, T. Wang, T. Kim, L. Lu, and L. Wenke. 2015. "Preventing Use-after-Free with Dangling Pointers Nullification." In *Network and Distributed Systems Security (NDSS)*.

Lewis, N., A. Case, A. Ali-Gombe, and G. G. Richard III. 2018. "Memory Forensics and the Windows Subsystem for Linux." *Digital Investigation* 26: S3–S11.

Ligh, M. H., A. Case, J. Levy, and A. Walters. 2014. *The Art of Memory Forensics: Detecting Malware and Threats in Windows, Linux, and Mac Memory.* Wiley.

Luceri, L., A. Deb, A. Badawy, and E. Ferrara. 2019. "Red Bots Do It Better: Comparative Analysis of Social Bot Partisan Behavior." In *Companion Proceedings of the 2019 World Wide Web Conference*, 1007–12.

Maisuradze, G., M. Backes, and C. Rossow. 2016. "What Cannot Be Read, Cannot Be Leveraged? Revisiting Assumptions of JIT-ROP Defenses." *USENIX Security* 16: 139–56.

Marco-Gisbert, H., and I. Ripoll. 2014. "On the Effectiveness of Full-ASLR on 64-bit Linux." In *Proceedings of the In-Depth Security Conference*.

Martindale, J. 2018. "From Pranks to Nuclear Sabotage, This Is the History of Malware." *Digitaltrends.* March 29. www.digitaltrends.com/computing/history-of-malware.

Marczak, B., and J. Scott-Railton. 2016. "NSO Group's iPhone Zero-days Used against a UAE Human Rights Defender." citizenlab.ca/2016/08/million-dollar-dissident-iphone-zero-day-nso-group-uae/.

MITRE Corporation. 2019. "Persistence, Tactic TA0003." attack.mitre.org/tactics/TA0003/.

Nagy, L. 2019. "Exploring emotet, an Elaborate Everyday Enigma." *Virus Bulletin.* www.virusbulletin.com/virusbulletin/2019/10/vb2019-paper-exploring-emotet-elaborate-everyday-enigma/.

Neumann, J. V. 1966. *Theory of Self-Replicating Automata.* University of Illinois Press. 63–78.

O'Donnell, L. 2020. "Emotet Now Hacks Nearby Wi-Fi Networks to Spread like a Worm." *threatpost.* threatpost.com/emotet-now-hacks-nearby-wi-fi-networks-to-spread-like-a-worm/152725/.

Onarlioglu, K., L. Bilge, A. Lanzi, D. Balzarotti, and E. Kirda. 2010. "G-Free: Defeating Return-Oriented Programming Through Gadget-less Binaries." In *Proceedings of the 26th Annual Computer Security Applications Conference*, 49–58.

Park, S., M. Specter, N. Narua, and R. L. Rivest. 2021. "Going from Bad to Worse: From Internet Voting to Blockchain Voting." *Journal of Cybersecurity* 7(1). academic.oup.com/cybersecurity/article/7/1/tyaa025/6137886.

Paruchuri, S., A. Case, and G. G. Richard III. 2020. "Gaslight Revisited: Efficient and Powerful Fuzzing of Digital Forensics Tools." In *Computers and Security* 97: 101986.

Pastrana, S., and G. Suarez-Tangil. 2019. "A First Look at the Cryptomining Malware Ecosystem: A Decade of Unrestricted Wealth." *In Proceedings of the Internet Measurement Conference,* 73–86.

Prenaud, K., S. Flowerday, M. Warkentin, P. Cockshott, and C. Orgeron. 2018. "Is the Responsibilization of the Cyber Security Risk Reasonable and Judicious?" *Computers and Security* 78: 198–211.

Prince, B. 2014. "'Syrian Malware Team' Uses BlackWorm RAT in Attacks." www.securityweek.com/syrian-malware-team-uses-blackworm-rat-attacks/.

Rashid, F.Y. 2019. "Disinformation Attacks Aren't Just against Elections." August 29. *Decipher.* duo.com/decipher/disinformation-attacks-aren-t-just-against-elections.

Reuters. 2019. "Uzbek Spies Attacked Dissidents with Off-the-Shelf Hacking Tools." www.reuters.com/article/idUSKBN1W1oZF/.

Richard, G. G., III. 2010. "Kernel Version-independent Tools for Deep, Live Digital Forensics." *Proceedings of the 66th Annual Meeting of the American Academy of Forensic Sciences (AAFS).*

⸻, and I. Ahmed. 2014. "Compressed RAM and Live Forensics." *Proceedings of the 66th Annual Meeting of the American Academy of Forensic Sciences (AAFS).*

⸻, and V. Roussev. 2005. "Scalpel: A Frugal, High Performance File Carver." *Digital Forensics Research Conference (DFRWS),* 71–77.

Ruiz, M. 2019. "The Changing Landscape of Disinformation and Cybersecurity Threats: A Recap from Verify 2019." May 2. Hewlett Foundation. hewlett.org/the-changing-landscape-of-disinformation-and-cybersecurity-threats-a-recap-from-verify-2019/.

Saltaformaggio, B., R. Bhatia, Z. Zhang, D. Xu, and G. G. Richard III. 2016. "Screen after Previous Screens: Spatial-temporal Recreation of Android App Displays from Memory Images." In *USENIX Security.*

Scott-Railton, J., B. Marczak, B. A. Razzak, M. Crete-Nishihata, and R. Deibert. 2017. "Senior Mexican Legislators and Politicians Targets with NSO Spyware." citizenlab.ca/2017/06/more-mexican-nso-targets/.

Seals, T. 2020. "Hackers Using Coronavirus Scare to Spread Emotet Malware in Japan." threatpost.com/coronavirus-propagate-emotet/152404/.

Shahmirza, A. 2019. "High Performance Fuzz Testing of Memory Forensics Frameworks." MS thesis, Louisiana State University.

Skape and Skywing. 2005. *Uninformed* 2(4). www.uninformed.org/?v=2&a=4.

Skape and J. Turkulainen. 2004. "Remote Library Injection." www.hick.org/code/skape/papers/remote-library-injection.pdf.

Song, W., H. Yin, C. Liu, and D. Song. 2018. "Deepmem: Learning Graph Neural Network Models for Fast and Robust Memory Forensic Analysis." In *Proceedings of the 2018 ACM SIGSAC Conference on Computer and Communications Security,* 606–18.

Spadafora, A. 2020. "Major Data Breach Exposes Database of 200 Million Users."
March 20. *TechRadar.* www.techradar.com/news/major-data-breach-exposes-data
base-of-200-million-users.

Steel, C. M. 2014. "Technical SODDI defenses: The Trojan Horse Defense Revisited."
Journal of Digital Forensics, Security and Law 9(4).

Swinhoe, D. and M. Hill. 2022. "The 15 Biggest Data Breaches of the 21st Century."
CSO Online. www.csoonline.com/article/2130877/the-biggest-data-breaches-of
-the-21st-century.html.

Sylve, J., A. Case, L. Marziale, and G. G. Richard III. 2012. "Acquisition and Analysis of
Volatile Memory from Android Devices." *Digital Investigation* 8(3).

Syverson, P., R. Dingledine, and N. Mathewson. 2004. "Tor: The Second Generation
Onion Router." In *Proceedings of Usenix Security,* 303–20.

TargetSmart. 2020. "Covid-19 and Elections—Findings from a National Poll of
American Voters." April 19. *TargetSmart.* insights.targetsmart.com/covid-19-and
-elections-findings-from-a-national-poll-of-american-voters.html.

Tolosana, R., R. Vera-Rodriguez, J. Fierrez, A. Morale, and J. Ortega-Garcia. 2020.
"Deepfakes and Beyond: A Survey of Face Manipulation and Fake Detection."
arXiv preprint. arXiv:2001.00179.

Tung, L. 2020. "Home Router Warning: They're Riddled with Known Flaws and Run
Ancient, Unpatched Linux." *ZDNet.* www.zdnet.com/article/home-router-warning
-theyre-riddled-with-known-flaws-and-run-ancient-unpatched-linux/.

Tziakouris, G. 2018. "Cryptocurrencies—A Forensic Challenge or Opportunity for Law
Enforcement? An INTERPOL Perspective." *IEEE Security and Privacy* 16(4): 92–94.

U.S. Office of Personnel Management. 2019. "Cybersecurity Incidents." www.opm.gov
/cybersecurity/cybersecurity-incidents/.

U.S. Senate Select Committee on Intelligence. 2019. *Russian Active Measures Campaigns and Interference in the 2016 U.S. election,* vol. 2: *Russia's Use of Social Media
with Additional Views.* www.intelligence.senate.gov/sites/default/files/documents
/Report_Volume2.pdf.

Verdoliva, L. 2020. "Media Forensics and Deepfakes: An Overview." *arXiv* preprint.
arXiv:2001.06564.

Volexity. 2016. "PowerDuke: Widespread Post-election Spear-phishing Campaigns Targeting Think Tanks and NGOs." www.volexity.com/blog/2016/11/09/powerduke
-post-election-spear-phishing-campaigns-targeting-think-tanks-and-ngos/.

Voolf, D., and R. Cohen. 2020. "Mirai COVID Variant Disregards Stay-at-Home Or-
ders." April 24. *F5 Labs.* www.f5.com/labs/articles/threat-intelligence/mirai-covid
-variant-disregards-stay-at-home-orders.

Weidenbach, P., and J. vom Dorp. 2020. "Home Router Security Report." *Fraunhofer*

FKIE. www.fkie.fraunhofer.ed/content/dam/fkie/de/documents/HomeRouter /HomeRouterSecurity_2020_Bericht.pdf.

Wikipedia. 2020. "List of Data Breaches." en.wikipedia.org/wiki/List_of_data_breaches #cite_note-135.

Zantout, B., and R. Haraty. 2011. "I2P Data Communication System." In *Proceedings of ICN: the Tenth International Conference on Networks,* 401–9.

If We Dare to Compare, Is Disinformation Being Spread to Elections Everywhere?

U.S. and Danish National Elections

• • •

JACOB GROSHEK AND SANDER ANDREAS SCHWARTZ

Before eventually becoming prime minister of the United Kingdom, Boris Johnson was scheduled to appear in court on allegations that, according to the *Guardian,* he "lied and misled" the public during the Brexit debate (Quinn 2019). The notion of politicians steering public opinion based on a certain interpretation of facts is nothing new. To this point, the former president of the United States, Donald Trump, was impeached (for the first time) in December 2019, in this instance as the result of an ongoing scandal related to withholding support to the Ukraine. Relatedly, and the point of this study, are former President Trump's ongoing "fake news" allegations and "alternative facts" campaigns that began immediately after he took office (Groshek and Koc-Michalska 2017).

While these particular charges did not culminate in any substantial disciplinary actions for either Johnson or Trump, such as removal from office, they are nonetheless emblematic of just how pivotal all sorts of actors—*including government officials and public figures*—can be in driving the spread of disinformation to potentially influence not only public debate but also the outcome of campaigns and policy decisions. This exact activity of elected officials acting as so-called "useful idiots" in spreading misinformation was highlighted in the *New York Times* opinion video series *Operation Infektion* (Ellick and Westbrook 2018) precisely because of their political authority and ability to shape media agendas. While the *New York Times* piece focused, to some extent, on former president Trump, the study reported here is more concerned with how other actors, including politicians, experts, journalists, and nonhuman actors, enter the social media arena specifically focused on elections and become influential in directing news and information around candidates and issues.

Along these lines in the Danish context, it could be argued that Rasmus Paludan, leader of the political movement Stram Kurs (Hard Line) in Denmark, is imitating the same populist playbook of distorted facts, scapegoating, extreme nationalism, and racism that former president Trump has embraced. Adding to the intrigue here in our cross-national "most different" analysis (compare Groshek and Engelbert 2012) is that President Trump was rebuked in August 2019 by the Danish prime minister Mette Frederiksen of the Social Democrats on the proposed sale of Greenland to the United States.

This study, therefore, examines social media output in these two unique political contexts in order to develop a better understanding of how much and what types of disinformation may be entering into these interrelated political arenas, and to categorize which actors are actively cultivating or squelching (dis)information. While we would ideally like to incorporate analyses from the 2020 U.S. national elections, our timeline did not allow us to collect data immediately prior to that election day. Thus, for the time being, and to establish precedent in developing a useful framework, we comparatively model the 2018 U.S. midterm elections and the 2019 Danish general elections on social media.

We focus on Twitter, which, as a publicly open social media platform, has become the principal vehicle for populists like President Trump to perform their brand of public diplomacy and "double differentiation"

(Groshek and Engelbert 2012; Engelbert and Groshek 2014). Of course, social media have, broadly speaking, come to define the twenty-first century in innumerable ways and forms, from mundane and miniscule to revolutionary and transformative (Pew 2015). By being embedded in everyday life, social media—and Twitter in particular—have also changed the way individuals manage both personal and professional affairs, including decisions that can affect their political beliefs and decision-making.

Given its enormous impact on the political functioning of network societies, Twitter has become routine to study, but a lack of cross-national comparative research still persists, particularly in understanding election disinformation that may be propagated by various users in political social networks. This study makes a contribution to filling that gap, particularly with an eye toward expanding on the "useful idiot" conceptualization of political leaders.

The 2018 U.S. Midterm Election Campaign

The U.S. midterms occur every fourth year on the first Tuesday in November, following four-year national, presidential election cycle but in even years at the "middle" of the term of the sitting president. Over the course of history, midterms have varied drastically in not only their perceived importance but also their voter-participation levels. As shown by McDonald (2018), since 1945 there has been considerable variation in midterm turnout, which was at an all-time low by 2014, with just 36.4 percent of eligible voters (compare *PBS Newshour* 2014).

Following the 2016 election of Donald Trump, however, the 2018 midterm elections attracted the most participation of any midterm cycle since 1945 (McDonald 2018). Arguably, many citizens perceived more to be at stake, and voters turned out at 49 percent nationwide (Segers 2018). While this may not seem overwhelming, such levels are typically only achieved during presidential election years and seem to speak to not only the rise of Trump but also the Republican-controlled Senate and House of Representatives (Bucy, Groshek, and Zhang 2019).

In the 2018 midterms, of the contested elections across the Senate and the House of Representatives, the Republican Party increased its majority with a net gain of two seats. In a rather drastic reversal of the 2016 national elections, the Democratic Party won back the House of Representatives with a net gain of forty-one seats. At the state level, Democrats picked up seven governorships, though these have relatively less importance in the national political landscape.

Additionally—and perhaps related to the relatively large turnout—there were notable victories for candidates who were women, people of color, and/or LGBTQ, including Jared Polis of Colorado, the first openly gay governor elected to that office in the United States. The 2018 midterms were also notable for overall expansions of Medicaid and the legalization of marijuana in many states. Economic issues, such as tariffs introduced by President Trump, seemed to weigh substantially on voters as well (Schwarz and Fetzer 2019).

This raises a point that other scholars have advanced regarding the Trump presidency, which is his violation of political norms and the effects that have rippled throughout U.S. politics as a result (Boczkowski and Papacharissi 2018; Nussbaum 2018). To some extent, the chaos that has ensued following Trump's election was already cast as a crisis of democracy, even before the COVID-19 pandemic, and while both the 2018 midterm election and 2020 presidential election results repudiated his style of governance, that did not extend to the Senate, and those results have had profound implications for American democracy since—including, but not limited to, the eventual result of both impeachment proceedings against Trump.

The 2019 Danish Election Campaign

The Danish parliamentary election is held at least every fourth year. Within this time period, the sitting prime minister can announce an election at any time that will then usually take place between two to four weeks after announcement. The election in 2019 was announced on May 7, and the election day was June 5, which then defined the actual election-campaign period. The Danish political system is a multiparty arrangement with two large parties and several smaller and supporting parties. In the 2019 election, thirteen parties were on the ballot, including three new parties, from which ten parties managed to get seats in the parliament. The three new parties included two positioned farthest to the right in the Danish political spectrum, based on a shared anti-immigration agenda (Stram Kurs and Nye Borgerlige). Particularly the party Stram Kurs (Hard Line) has been highly controversial during the election. Party leader Rasmus Paludan has been notorious for his controversial and provocative behavior and rhetoric. As a result, many of the traditional parties have been highly critical of Rasmus Paludan by publicly rejecting his political discourse as well as his agenda.

The introduction of new right-wing parties showed some momentum for the extreme right-wing agenda leading up to the Danish election 2019, similarly to the political changes in many other European countries, including neighboring country Sweden. Ultimately, however, the right-wing agenda was overshadowed by other political agendas such as sustainable development and green politics as well as welfare politics. The populist right-wing party Dansk Folkeparti (Danish People's Party), the second largest party after the 2015 election, received less than half of the vote shares from 2015 in the 2019 election. Rasmus Paludan and his party, Stram Kurs, did not get enough votes to have a seat in the parliament, though Nye Borgerlige (New Right) did manage to get over the 2 percent threshold of votes, thereby earning four seats.

Because of controversial behavior and rhetoric, Rasmus Paludan was very successful at grabbing the attention of politicians and journalists during the election campaign. On social media the party profile and his personal profiles have been suspended or deactivated several times before, during, and after the election campaign. During the election he did have an active personal Twitter account, even though the party profile was suspended by Twitter. After the election campaign, however, his personal profile was also suspended. Furthermore, Rasmus Paludan is currently in court charged for counts of racism and libel, partly based on his behavior during the election campaign in 2019.

Having outlined the background of these two political campaigns and national cultures, we propose the following research questions:

RQ1—How do network analyses of tweets that mention the campaigns compare in terms of volume, density, and user influence?

RQ2—Which categories of users are most influential in structuring (dis)information flows on Twitter, and can significant differences be observed?

RQ3—What interpretations can be made by comparing these unique political contexts to better understand disinformation as a global phenomenon?

Methods

Data collection for this project took place across two separate installations (one hosted in the United States and one hosted in Denmark) of the Digital Methods Initiative—Twitter Collection and Analysis Toolkit (DMI-TCAT), which allows media researchers to collect tweets off the STREAM API (application programming interface) on an ongoing basis. Working from the so-called "gardenhose" access to the Twitter API, the DMI-TCAT adds a computational interface layer over that raw data and processes it for network analysis and visualization in Gephi or other similar applications. With this software, social data in the millions of units are quickly and easily sorted by algorithms to find users or items of importance on Twitter.

The DMI-TCAT does not provide full firehose access to all historical tweets. Rather, it returns a generally representative sample of content from the freely available STREAM API that includes a variable number of tweets on any given topic, relatively to the total volume of tweets being posted at any given time (Gerlitz and Rieder 2013; Groshek and Tandoc 2016). In short, while there are no guarantees of collecting every post on any given search topic, the DMI-TCAT has been well tested and reported on in many scholarly articles. In the cases reported here, we do not claim full representation but rather satisfactory generalizability of Twitter data.

For more details on the DMI-TCAT and its operation, we encourage readers to visit its github page (github.com/digitalmethodsinitiative/dmi-tcat) and note that this cloud-based analytics program is free and customizable for anyone wishing to use it. We therefore also offer our sincere thanks to the developers, Erik Borra and Bernhard Rieder, for their tireless efforts (compare Borra and Rieder 2014).

The Twitter API that powered the DMI-TCAT at the time the analyses were conducted has since been decommissioned (and Twitter itself has been rebranded as "X" under Elon Musk's new ownership). Digital data access—especially free access—has long had barriers of many kinds, which have included expertise, coding, storage, terms of service, and now more than ever, cost. Indeed, social media research has now entered the paid-API era, and it is unlikely that hundreds of millions of tweets or any other user-generated content will be freely available again in the future.

Still, there is a variety of organizations and nonprofits, such as DiscoverText (discovertext.com), the Social Media Research Foundation (www.smrfoundation.org), and the Institute for Representation in Society and Media (www.irsm.io) that are working to maintain access to large volumes of social media data and leading analytic tools for academic researchers at marginal costs for subscriptions or free trial access.

Data Collection for the 2018 U.S. Midterm Elections

For the 2018 U.S. midterm elections, we chose one month's worth of Twitter data immediately before and briefly after the elections took place on November 6, 2018. This window of thirty days from October 11 through November 11 of course does not account for all the variation that could have taken place over the course of the campaigns but nonetheless highlights a crucial period in the election cycle when coverage would have been most heightened, and that has been the focal point for past studies of social media and election coverage (Groshek and Groshek 2013; Groshek and Al-Rawi 2013). We included an additional five days after election day because a number of elections were contested, and vigorous discussions continued on social media in connection with those outcomes.

We entered the following search terms into our DMI-TCAT to be as comprehensive as possible in collecting relevant data: #2018midterms, #election, #midterm, #november2018, or #vote2018. With these search parameters, we were able to gather 156,641 tweets from 99,750 distinct users during this month-long period.

Data Collection for the 2019 Danish General Elections

To create as much of an apples-to-apples comparison as possible, we similarly collected tweets for the Danish general elections for a period of one month leading up and including the day of the election. The Danish elections do not follow a set schedule like the United States, so the campaign period being compared is considerably shorter. In this sense, we can argue that we have collected Twitter data for the entire period of this election, with May 5 to June 5, 2019, set as our dates of coverage.

As with the U.S. election, we set relatively wide linguistic operationalizations to our keyword-based search to collect data for the Danish case. Based on the expertise of one of our Danish authors, here we employed the following search terms: #ft19, #ft2019, #ftvalg, #ftvalg19, #ftvalg2019, #fv19, #fv2019, #valg19, or #valg2019. Following these search parameters, the DMI-TCAT system collected a total of 38,127 tweets from 8,662 distinct users during this month-long period roughly equivalent to the U.S. midterms from the previous year in leading up to both elections.

As part of our process to examine the research questions posed, we worked independently with data derived from two of the separate DMI-TCAT systems outlined above to generate co-mention network files of nodes and edges. These were then used to sort Twitter users visually and algorithmically from both elections using Gephi, an open-source data-visualization program specializing in network analysis. As the focus of our comparative approach was to model user influence in each of these datasets, we calculated evenly comparable metrics of betweenness centrality as well as community detection (as determined using the modularity algorithm). Additionally, we spatialized the networks using the same force-directed layout process known as Open Ord.

The betweenness-centrality algorithm was calculated for each corpus of election tweets to measure the frequency of a user node appearing on the shortest path between other nodes present in the network (Groshek and Al-Rawi 2015; Groshek and Tandoc 2016). This algorithm thereby models "influence" as a function of identifying users acting as gatekeepers passing messages through the networks of users mentioning each election. In short, larger nodes are more influential in moving messages through the network to diverse user communities, which are identified by the colors of the nodes determined by applying the modularity algorithm to each election corpus (Blondel et al. 2008). As noted by Groshek and Tandoc (2016), "Smaller nodes refer to users who were less active in mentioning and being mentioned by others" (204).

Once the betweenness-centrality scores were determined, we rank ordered these values and then coded one hundred "most-between" users from each dataset. These rankings were used to select the top one hundred: accounts for each of the samples, which were then manually coded into expert, media, citizen, and political party based on their profile descriptions, bio statements, and related information (compare Groshek and Tandon 2016 for similar categorizations). Users were also coded for likelihood of being a real user or a bot (compare Al-Rawi, Groshek and Zhang 2018), political leanings, and more specific roles in organizations that were disclosed (such as a political party candidate or official).

These categorizations are based on past work and provide vital insight into the nature of users sharing (mis)information about these elections. In short, while some of these operationalizations are still exploratory, especially in the case of estimating bot (or nonhuman, algorithmic, or cyborg) accounts, on the whole, they make it possible to compare the engagement of different stakeholders in communicating about these two unique campaigns.

Findings

In addressing our three research questions, we begin by unpacking findings for each national context and then bringing comparative points to bear. In doing so, we can examine key metrics of volume, density, and user influence with key categorizations across the campaigns that help us to arrive at a better understanding of disinformation in comparative political communication contexts.

The 2018 U.S. Midterm Elections

In beginning our analyses, we created a network graph of user mentions for the 2018 midterm elections. When categorizing those users by baseline metrics, we observed an overwhelmingly high percentage of citizens as influential actors in mentioning other users to pass messages through the network. Indeed, when ranked by betweenness-centrality scores, 63 percent of the most influential users in this network were self-identified as citizens. Beyond that, there was an equivalent tie between experts and media-affiliated users at 10 percent. Political parties rounded out the baseline user profiles at just 6 percent, and there were 11 percent of the most influential accounts (by betweenness centrality) that were deleted and/or suspended by the time of analysis, suggesting they were either bots or they violated Twitter's terms of service (ToS). These findings are summarized in table 1.

Based on these rankings and categorization system, it seems that citizen activists are leading figures in the U.S. midterm elections. This, however, would be somewhat misleading, as thirteen of the most influential users by betweenness centrality were secondarily categorized as "citizen" conservative bot account. In other words, the user accounts of pinkk91over, zeusfanhouse, oceanpatriot9, g1rly_tattooed, chrisconsrv1776, _iamanita_d, lastnamefree, aldrpeg4, traderjohnt1, doodisgirl, buzzman888, cb618444, and gbroh10 all exhibited automated behaviors and characteristics that would make them very likely to be bots, not human users (Al-Rawi, Groshek, and Zhang 2018).

Table 1. Percentages for baseline user profile characteristics of 100 "most influential" users by betweenness centrality in tweets about the U.S. midterms and the Danish general elections

	U.S. Midterms	Danish General Elections
Citizens	63%	39%
Experts	10%	14%
Media	10%	18%
Political parties	6%	27%
Deleted/suspended	11%	2%

Note: Percentages reported here are for the top 100 users for each month-long period as sorted by betweenness centrality scores: ($\chi2$ (df: 4) = 28.19, p < .001).

Altogether, these findings suggest that the U.S. Twittersphere on the midterm elections was, at least on the surface, horizontal and participatory, but more to the point, it was polluted with hyperpartisan bot accounts amplifying dubious messages, often from one another. In terms of corrective balance, liberal human users are the next most prominent overall, but the first of those accounts—co_rapunze14 and kikiadine—registered as the thirty-seventh and thirty-eighth most influential accounts that were not organizations or presumed bots. Following the foxfriendsfirst show at sixty-fifth most influential by betweenness centrality, the most influential journalist was jeremyscahill, founder of *The Intercept,* ranked at seventh-third in betweenness centrality in covering the midterm elections.

These findings thus paint a complex picture of horizontal and participatory debate, and there is very limited engagement by politicians or political parties with any other users communicating on social media about this election. The most engaged politician in this corpus was Bob Hugin, who ran unsuccessfully for office in New Jersey during the midterm election. The only other two politicians among the most influential one hundred as ranked by betweenness centrality were Robyn Vining, who was elected to the Wisconsin State Assembly, and Lindsey Graham, the U.S. senator from South Carolina, who won reelection.

Put bluntly, the discussion of the 2018 U.S. midterm elections was overrun with ersatz "citizen" conservative bot accounts and relatively little else to moderate those messages. While looking at the overall percentages, as in table 2 below, it seems that NGOs and other experts weighed in to strike a sort of organic balance, but these accounts were relatively marginal among the most influential accounts, and journalists and news organizations were all but absent. This suggests that the useful idiots in this social media coverage were the nonhuman users programmed to be precisely that, and nearly no actors stood up as corrective mechanisms in response, at least insofar as that can be captured through mentioning activity, which is a limitation to these analyses.

The 2019 Danish National Elections

As summarized in table 1, the Danish Twitter debate surrounding the election campaign included a surprisingly high number of citizens as the most influential and a surprisingly low number of legacy media actors. The top one hundred most influential according to betweenness-centrality scores included 39 percent citizens, 27 percent politicians or political parties, 18 percent legacy media or media celebrities, and 14 percent professional experts—mostly lobbyists and academics. Even in the top ten there are still four citizens present as the most central and influential actors in the network. Overall, this suggests that the Danish Twittersphere allows for a very horizontal and participatory debate with multiple actors outside of the parliamentary sphere. Even though it is more difficult to identify the citizen profiles according to a binary liberal or conservative logic, it does seem that both sides are represented in both the top ten and top one hundred most influential, showing signs of political diversity as well.

The Danish election campaign introduced new political parties into the mix—most notably the highly controversial politician Rasmus Paludan, who established the far-right party Firm Line leading up to the 2019 election. Even though the party did not end up with any seats in parliament, Paludan's profile was prominently positioned in the network as a key influential character. This was most likely based on the controversial nature of his political viewpoints and provocative dialogue. Based on the betweenness-centrality score, he is the fourth most influential profile in the network during the campaign. His party profile is not in the top one hundred because it was suspended by Twitter just before the election for violation of terms of service. Briefly after the Danish election, his own profile was also removed, yet it remained visible and active throughout the campaign.

The most influential profile, according to betweenness centrality, was one of the smaller parties, the Social-Liberal Party; and the party leader, Morten Østergaard, was the third most influential. Another small party, the Alternative, which promoted a green and sustainable agenda, was in the top ten most influential list. These three minor parties (Stram Kurs, Radikale Venstre, and Alternativet) in Danish politics managed to get a central position in the Twitter debate, showing potential for increased visibility of the smaller parties in the newer social media platforms.

However, this may also introduce disproportional visibility to fringe political opinions such as those of Rasmus Paludan. Yet his central position is likely due to the controversial manner of his rhetoric. Interestingly, and perhaps indicative of the findings in the Danish context, the prime minister at the time (Lars Løkke Rasmussen) was not even in the top ten but rather the fourteenth most influential profile. His party, the Liberal Party, was placed twelfth, and the Social Democratic Party, the competing and largest party in Denmark, was number fifteen. The current prime minister from the Social Democratic Party did not have a Twitter profile during the 2019 election.

Comparative Analyses

A comparison of the two data archives shows that the U.S. midterms generated more traffic from a larger number of unique users. However, the relative number of posts per unique user was 4.40 for the Danish elections and just 1.57 posts per unique user for the U.S. midterms and, thus, the cleavages between the two elections are readily apparent, even at a very high level, where the volume of posts alone is not solely indicative of user engagement.

Table 2. Percentages for additional user profile characteristics of 100 "most influential" users by betweenness centrality in tweets about the U.S. midterms and the Danish general elections

	U.S. Midterms	Danish General Elections
"Citizen" conservative bots	40%	—
Liberal human users	11%	23%
Neutral human users	—	5%
Conservative human users	5%	9%
"Citizen" liberal bots	4%	—
Journalists (right and/or left)	6%	9%
Politicians (right and/or left)	3%	18%
NGOs and experts	10%	14%
Explicit bots	—	2%
Other (including deleted)	21%	20%

Note: Percentages reported here are for the top 100 users for each month-long period as sorted by betweenness-centrality scores; (χ2 (df: 9) = 68.38, p < .001; some cells have fewer than 5 minimum observed values.

Notably, networks were much denser in Denmark, despite fewer posts and far fewer users, suggesting more "broadcasting" instead of engaging in the United States. Findings suggest cultural differences in use and interaction style; politicians and media actors in Denmark are far more influential in communicating with other users.

There are also drastic differences in user types across the two countries, particularly of nonhuman agents, which are dominant in the United States and nearly absent in Denmark. These findings alone do not prove disinformation flows but do indicate a greater likelihood of the discursive space being amplified and tilting far to the right wing in the United States, specifically through bots masquerading as citizens. Indeed, fourteen of the top fifteen most influential users in the United

States were right-wing "citizen" bot accounts, of which none were detected in the Danish context, but where bots were explicitly identified as political bot accounts deployed with the stated purpose of retweeting Danish election information.

In the U.S. case, this is largely being directed by conservative bot accounts with little offset by liberal human accounts and NGOs or other experts. In Denmark, politicians have chosen to lead, and messages are countervailed more evenly by liberal human users and greater proportion of NGOs and other experts. These results are summarized in table 2.

Pathways to Participation, Disinformation, or Both?

We modeled and compared the relative influence of particular users—whether government officials themselves or other types of human and automated users—to better understand potential disinformation flows in two elections. We operationalized not only how candidates and government officials negotiate their behaviors in these campaigns on social media but also how effective the campaigns are. The findings suggest that Danish politicians interact with other users far more than their American counterparts and reveal the extent to which they spread disinformation. Building on previous research, we leverage the Digital Methods Initiative—Twitter Collection and Analysis Toolkit (DMI-TCAT) to collect and model social media data to identify influential users and disinformation sources and flows around these campaigns.

Results from these analyses suggest that the ongoing evolution of networked gatekeeping has a relative dearth of journalists and news organizations participating in social media coverage, in this case elections in the United States and Denmark. While media organizations can still better leverage affordances in social networks, such as @mentions and following, there are substantial differences across these contexts, with implications for the flow of disinformation in which journalists and media organizations represented just 10 percent in the U.S. and 18 percent in Denmark of the most influential users on Twitter.

There seems to be an organic balancing out of viewpoints in Denmark, with far fewer automated accounts, and while "citizens" are prominent gatekeepers in both nations, political parties are noticeably absent in the United States. Whether or not that could exacerbate misinformation is a standing question, but it is noteworthy that only 3 percent of the most influential accounts were for U.S. politicians whereas that figure was 18 percent in Denmark. These findings point to uniquely adapted affordance effects (Groshek and Tandoc 2016), where gatekeeping has been renegotiated by non-journalists, citizens, bots, political parties, and experts that have been starkly divided and differently negotiated across these political, national, and cultural contexts.

In conclusion, while the Danish general election seems more balanced in left / right political actors, there is no guarantee of those actors squelching misinformation, specifically based on the tendency of populist politicians to distort truth claims and fan divisions via social media. The discursive election spaces in both countries desperately demand more input by media organizations and journalists as expert cullers of facts. While the notion of citizen journalism has certainly expanded with the proliferation of mobile phone–based social media, the "crowd" cannot replace news organizations with professionalized routines. Moreover, the concept of citizens is certainly being redefined by bot accounts in the United States specifically, and whether human, cyborg, or bot, users have the capability to artificially shift debate by their performative actions on Twitter.

As the field continues to evolve, the demand for journalists who post on social media and assert themselves more into the conversation is absolutely essential. While platform regulation can be a public good, such as when Twitter added a fact-check to several of President Trump's tweets (Conger and Isaac 2020) and ultimately banned him from the platform, it is often too little and too late. Failing a more robust mechanism, the public sphere being cultivated in these different contexts is dangerously exposed to disinformation and appropriation via their own distinct cultural adaptations.

Al-Rawi, A., J. Groshek, and L. Zhang. 2018. "What the Fake? Assessing the Extent of Networked Political Spamming and Bots in the Propagation of #fakenews on Twitter." *Online Information Review.*

Blondel, V. D., J. Guillaume, R. Lambiotte, and E. Lefebvre. 2008. "Fast Unfolding of Communities in Large Networks." *Journal of Statistical Mechanics,* 10.

Boczkowski, P. J., and Z. Papacharissi. 2018. *Trump and the Media.* MIT Press.

Borra, E., and B. Rieder. 2014. "Programmed Method: Developing a Toolset for Capturing and Analyzing Tweets." *Asian Journal of Information Management* 66 (3): 262–78. doi:10.1108/AJIM-09-2013-0094.

Bucy, E., J. Groshek, and L. Zhang. 2019. "Evolving Support of the Media Participation Hypothesis: Evidence from Midterms Elections in 2014 and 2018." Manuscript presented at AEJMC Annual Conference, Detroit.

Chadwick, A. (2017). *The Hybrid Media System: Politics and Power.* 2nd ed. Oxford University Press.

Conger, K. and M. Isaac. 2020. "Defying Trump, Twitter Doubles Down on Labeling Tweets." *New York Times.* www.nytimes.com/2020/05/28/technology/trump-twitter -fact-check.html.

Ellick, A., and A. Westbrook. 2018. "Operation Infektion." *New York Times.* www.nytimes .com/2018/11/12/opinion/russia-meddling-disinformation-fake-news-elections .html.

Engelbert, J., and J. Groshek. 2014. "Populism as PR: An International Perspective of Public Diplomacy Trends. In G. Golan, S. Yang, and D. Kinsey, eds., *International Public Relations and Public Diplomacy: Communication and Engagement,* 331–45. Peter Lang.

Gerlitz, C., and B. Rieder, B. 2013. "Mining One Percent of Twitter: Collections, Baselines, Sampling." *M/C Journal* 16 (2).

Groshek, J., and A. Al-Rawi. 2013. "Public Sentiment and Critical Framing in Social Media Content during the 2012 U.S. Presidential Campaign." *Social Science Computer Review* 31 (5): 563–76.

Groshek, J., and A. Al-Rawi. 2015. "Anti-Austerity in the Euro Crisis: Modeling Protest with Online-Mobile-Social Media, Usage, Users and Content." *International Journal of Communication* 9: 3280–3303.

Groshek, J., M. Basil, L. Guo, S. Parker Ward, F. Farraye, and J. Reich. 2017. "Social Media, Social Stigma: An Examination of Media Consumption and Creation in Attitudes toward and Knowledge of Inflammatory Bowel Disease." *Journal of Medical Internet Research* 19 (12): 1–10.

Groshek, J., E. Bucy, and L. Zhang. 2018. "Evolving Support of the Media Participation Hypothesis: Evidence from Midterms Elections in 2014 and 2018." Manuscript presented to AEJMC Annual Conference, Toronto.

Groshek, J., and J. Engelbert. 2012. "A Cross-National Comparison of Populist Political Movements and Media Uses in the United States and the Netherlands." *New Media and Society* 15 (2): 183–202.

Groshek, J., and M. K. Groshek. 2013. "Agenda Trending: Reciprocity and the Predictive Capacity of Social Networking Sites in Intermedia Agenda Setting across Topics over Time." *Media and Communication* 1 (1). doi.10.17645/mac.viii.71.

Groshek, J., and K. Koc-Michalska. 2017. "Helping Populism Win? Social Media Use, Filter Bubbles, and Support for Populist Presidential Candidates in the 2016 U.S. Election Campaign." *Information Communication and Society* 20 (9): 1389–1407.

Groshek, J., and E. Tandoc. 2016. "The Affordance Effect: Gatekeeping and (Non)Reciprocal Journalism on Twitter." *Computers in Human Behavior* 66: 201–10.

Nussbaum, M. C. 2018. *The monarchy of Fear: A Philosopher Looks at Our Political Crisis.* Simon and Schuster.

PBS Newshour. 2014. "2014 Midterm Election Turnout Lowest in 70 years." November 10. www.pbs.org/newshour/politics/2014-midterm-election-turnout-lowest-in-70 -years.

Pew Research Center. 2015. "The evolving role of news on Twitter and Facebook." July. pewrsr.ch/1M8rcq2.

Quinn, B. 2019. "Boris Johnson to Appear in Court over Brexit Misconduct Claims." May 29. *The Guardian.* amp.theguardian.com/politics/2019/may/29/boris-johnson -appear-court-eu-referendum-misconduct-claims.

Schwarz, C., and T. Fetzer. 2019. "Tariffs and Politics: Evidence from Trump's Trade Wars." *Social Science Research Network.* SSRN 3349000.

Segers, G. 2018. "Record Voter Turnout In 2018 Midterm Elections." November 7. *CBS News.* www.cbsnews.com/news/record-voter-turnout-in-2018-midterm-elections/.

"Voting Eligible Population Turnout in U.S. Midterm Elections." Sources: 1946–2014: National General Election VEP Turnout Rates, 1789–Present. Michael McDonald. 2018 November General Election Turnout Rates www.electproject.org/national -1789-present (accessed November 12, 2018 [estimate]). Michael McDonald. www .electproject.org/2018g (accessed January 7, 2019).

Generation "Fake News"

Young Voters' Responses to Disinformation

• • •

JAKOB OHME

The first digital native citizens are coming of age in a time when disinformation is an everyday part of political communication activities. Much will depend on how this new generation responds to information that is spread as truthful yet later turns out to be inaccurate. The term "fake news" is outdated in an academic context and has been co-opted by the people who are trying to traffic in misinformation to delegitimize factually correct information. Yet, in society—and not least the youngest cohorts—it is still widely used and has thereby the potential to shape a generation's understanding of trust in the media.

Young citizens' political socialization—understood as a process by which a person forms a basic understanding of the norms and practices of the political system—thereby determines how this new generation deals with the communication routines they grow up with. Experiencing one's formative years in an age of disinformation can, therefore, bear risks for the future of democracy. Will Generation Z voters perceive it as normal that people hold their own truth and find supporting information online, or will they turn out to be hypercritical toward every information piece presented to them, thereby contributing to further mitigation of legacy media's role in informing the public? Generational gaps, as they exist in the use of news and political engagement (see Andersen et al. 2022), could also become a reality in trust in news and journalism (see also Brosius, Ohme, and de Vreese 2021).

This essay will discuss the likelihood of these and other scenarios by building on political socialization literature. In light of recent empirical work on youth mobilization, it will explore how young voters' democratic actions might be shaped by the omnipresence of disinformation. Eventually, the essay will present an outlook on how a society and its institutions can help young citizens to navigate the digital media environment despite the threat of disinformation.

Growing Up around Misinformation

There never is a good time for disinformation, but for today's young voters —the first digital natives that are entering the electorate—the surge of disinformation comes at an especially unfortunate time. Growing up is difficult in many regards: society expects young citizens to determine their identities, choose what paths to pursue in life, and select peers and partners to do so with, learn about fundamental societal norms, start informing themselves about political developments, and ultimately make informed vote decisions in their first elections.

In a post-truth age, this task becomes increasingly difficult. Most citizens in western societies nowadays are aware that disinformation— defined as information spread with the goal of deception—presents a problem for society (Hameleers et al. 2020). However, experiences on how to tackle its spread and guidance on how to detect fake news—"a form of disinformation that mimics the look and feel of news" (Tandoc, Lim, and Ling 2019)—are still sparse. For young voters, this means they cannot simply take over accepted behaviors and strategies from their parents and teachers as they do when it comes to the political values of a society or moral norms. Rather, they are very much on their own to make sense of a media environment where it is now common to doubt information that is spread, where guiding journalistic principles such as truth and objectivity are crumbling, and where the intention behind a message often is more in focus than the message itself.

What does it mean for young citizens to grow up in an age of disinformation? How well are they prepared to detect fake news? And how will this young generation react to this new information environment and, thereby, shape the future and functioning of the political communication ecosystem? This essay approaches these questions by developing different scenarios and giving an outlook on how Generation Z may react to growing up between disinformation and fake news.

The Uncertain Young Voter in an Age of Disinformation

When it comes to navigating the political landscape, young voters are, in general, less certain than older citizens. Reasons for this are their lack of experience in using political information to form their own political decisions along with other guiding factors, such as satisfaction with the incumbent government or levels of party identification (Aalberg and Jenssen 2007; Colwell Quarles 1979; O'Keefe and Liu 1980). In the United States, almost half of the youngest generation of voters call themselves independents, a number much higher compared to older generations (Cohn and Caumont 2016; Doherty, Kiley, and O'Hea 2018). In countries with multiparty systems and less pronounced patterns of party identification in society, the number of people who lack a clear party identification is even lower (Nicholson et al. 2018). This lack of affiliation and experience can result in lower certainty about political issues. The first voters of Generation Z, for example, showed significantly lower certainty about whom to vote for in the 2015 Danish national election compared to older voters (Ohme, de Vreese, and Albæk 2018). At the same time, their certainty on issue positions about policy statements concerning immigration, economic impact on the environment, health care, and tax regulations was lower in all cases compared to experienced voters.

Less strong political opinions, as well as lower levels of party affiliation, make young voters open to additional guidance, whether to form a vote decision or, more generally, to navigate a political sphere that society now expects them to be part of. Media that provide them with political information are an indispensable source for most young voters to receive information about political developments, as is talking to their parents and peers (Aalberg and Jenssen 2007; Colwell Quarles 1979; Marquart, Ohme, and Möller 2020). But with a rapid change in the media ecology that young citizens grow up in, the role of the media as an information source for young voters is floundering. Lower levels and quality of political news, a higher fragmentation and polarization of the media environment, and changes in exposure patterns—such as inadvertent exposure (for example, Thorson 2020) or news snacking (for example, Ohme and Mothes 2023)—are within-system changes that contribute to an altered role of media as a guiding source in young citizens' political socialization (Van Aelst et al. 2017). More fundamentally, this essay looks at what role news media may play in informing prospective voters who are growing up in times where the core aspect of media— their reputation to report correct and unbiased information—is under attack. Useful or not, narratives about "fake news" directly connect the spread of mis- and disinformation with the promise that news media were (and very often still are) associated with—to report "real" news. But if young voters do not learn this association as an automatism, growing up in times of disinformation may have further consequences for them than becoming ill-informed on specific political issues.

Lance Bennett and Steve Livingstone (2018) suggest that a loss of trust in the democratic institutions of press and politics is at the core of reasons for what they call a growing disinformation order. This new order deeply affects political communication processes that form the basis of information proliferation that citizens ultimately act on in a democratic society. According to them, the combination of higher institutional trust and fewer media channels previously allowed for the distribution of political information. This information was then framed by legacy media to publics that acted on it. But with the proliferation of mostly digitally networked media channels and fragmentation of audiences, this standardized process of information distribution has become less relevant (see also Neuberger et al. 2023). The rise of networked media happened simultaneously with the rejection of core institutions. The subsequent demand for alternative information, that is, information that is not coming from the core institutions of press and politics themselves (Bennett and Livingstone 2018), could easily be met by a digital media environment in which each and everyone could disseminate information that had the look and feel of news (Schifferes et al. 2014). This combination of a growing rejection of political and media elites and the unrestricted spread of information due to the proliferation of digitally networked media is one core reason for the development of the disinformation order.

A second factor that has likely contributed to the prevalence of disinformation in today's media environment is the number of information channels growing so fast that most citizens have not developed the literacy to evaluate their quality and intentions. Especially when it comes to digital media literacy, older citizens may be worse off navigating digital news environments. Although it was not a prevalent behavior, in the 2016 U.S. election, citizens over sixty-five years were seven times more likely to share stories from domains that were associated with spreading fake news (Guess, Nagler, and Tucker 2019). In a slowly developing media environment, audiences had more time to adapt to new information offers and to learn and test whether a newspaper, TV broadcaster, or news website was trustworthy as compared to a fast-evolving digital media landscape. In a pre-digital age, trust in legacy news media was therefore comparably high. In the 1990s, almost half of U.S. citizens agreed that the press could be trusted (Hanitzsch, van Dalen, and Steindl 2018). This is partly because people could establish trust and routines to evaluate media over time. The rapid growth of media channels as a result of digitalization made this learning curve steeper and ultimately overburdened many citizens' abilities to distinguish whether a source of information was a legacy-media website, a clickbait site, or the blog post of a citizen or political actor. With too many sources to properly evaluate, a number of citizens decided to rely on information that had the look and feel of what they had formerly known as news (a publicly available news item with a headline, a teaser, a picture, or a video) and that fit their worldviews best. The sometimes-inconvenient truth disseminated by legacy media was replaced by the convenient post-truth of information. In 2014, less than a quarter of U.S. citizens said they trusted "the press" (Hanitzsch, van Dalen, and Steindl 2018), a number that may look even grimmer today. However, a growing number of people started to trust news websites outside the spectrum of legacy media. So while a decline in the trust in elites of politics and press may be a starting point of the disinformation order, citizens' (in)ability to deal with the steep increase of choice in news sources has likely contributed to what now has become an age of disinformation.

Back in 2016, only a fraction of users shared any stories on Facebook that were coming from a fake news account (Guess, Nagler, and Tucker 2019). In 2020, disinformation is one of the most prevalent topics discussed in connection with news media, and the perception of living in an age of disinformation has spread through societies quickly. An extensive analysis of levels of mis- and disinformation in ten European countries shows that the perception of the media as mis- and disinforming is widespread among citizens (Hameleers et al. 2021). In most countries surveyed, agreement to statements such as *"The news media do not report accurately on facts that happened,"* and *"The news media are deliberately lying to the people,"* is below the mean.

Today, about 50 percent of Americans perceive made-up news as a major problem in their country, ranking even before climate change, racism, and terrorism (Mitchell et al. 2019). Hence, the problem of disinformation has arrived in society and is, therefore, also likely to shape the way in which young voters rely on the media in their attempt to form vote decisions.

Five Responses of Young Voters to Disinformation

In the following section, potential responses of young voters to disinformation are discussed. Based on recent trends in the political and media environment, it is possible to derive indications of how realistic each of these responses is. The starting point of these thought experiments is the fact that, at a young age, voters rely strongly on information from the media to cast their votes. Hence, recent news-use patterns that young voters show and the extent to which they can make sense of the "disinformation order" will determine how the media shape their political participation in upcoming elections and in later stages of life. None of the following scenarios fully fits a specific electoral context or is likely to come true exactly as described. Rather, they are food for thought and can be helpful in supporting or preventing certain outcomes.

Young Voters Rely on Disinformation and Act on It

One possible response to growing up in an age of disinformation is that Generation Z voters could have no, or little, response at all. Young citizens have been politically socialized by the media and will continue to rely on political information that they receive in the current media environment for their electoral participation. In this scenario, young voters might care little about the possibility that information they receive may be factually incorrect or may have been produced to deceive citizens. They will continue to follow their learned information routines of receiving news mostly from social media platforms or online-only news sources before elections. To reduce uncertainty on how to cast their vote, young voters would keep their role as "cognitive misers," who focus on information that is appealing, easy to digest, and does not result in cognitive dissonance (Lau and Redlawsk 2001; Fiske and Taylor 1991). Their dealing with the media as an information source before an upcoming election would thereby not fundamentally differ compared to the strategies of previous generations (Colwell Quarles 1979; O'Keefe and Liu 1980). But, with the loss of the gatekeeping function of legacy media in the digital news environment, many young voters will ultimately be informed by the messages that reach them first, that are most illuminating, or that are most often repeated or supported in their social network. Although these young voters may to a lower extent seek "alternative information" that confirms preexisting beliefs compared to older citizens, social network sites' push-media logic (Klinger and Svensson 2015) and the possibility of microtargeting (Kim et al. 2018) may expose young people to information specifically designed to deceive them. In this scenario it is likely that forms of political participation—such as turning out or attending a demonstration—will at least partially rely on factually incorrect information.

Young Voters Rely on a Narrower Circle of News Sources

Young voters may show a higher uncertainty in what information they can trust. The widespread concerns about made-up information and the perception of disinformation in the media could make young citizens aware of the possibility of being disinformed. In other words, at an age where young voters need information to inform themselves politically, they may perceive gathering information as more risky than beneficial. To minimize the risk of being disinformed, in this second scenario, young voters would rely on a narrow circle of news. They will not fully waive being informed by the media: for one reason, because society still expects them to inform themselves, and second, because they are at a phase when many of them want to make up their minds independently. However, they will do so by relying on a more manageable amount of information.

One way for young voters to achieve this is to hold on to informational sources they know well and with which they have already established some level of trust (Matsa et al. 2018). However, before they reach voting age, young citizens show lower levels of news use (Bhatti and Hansen 2012). Hence, in many cases, the number of sources they know and have established a relationship with is small, and the diversity of information these sources provide is restricted. Social media—the platforms from which today's first-time voters receive most of their news—to some extent provide fertile ground for such behavior and retraction from unknown sources. The algorithmic pre-filtering on these platforms can be used as a tool to keep information networks small and selective. On social media platforms, it is possible to actively curate one's media diet by selecting and deselecting information sources, or to curate it unconsciously by recurrently engaging with a small number of information sources. In addition, social filtering can help young voters to follow news that is supported, or that receives increased attention, in their peer networks (Marquart, Ohme, and Möller 2020). Thus a small number of news sources "borrow the trust" from young voters' social network and make it to their narrow circles of news while the general stream of information passes by. Cotter and Thorson (2022) find that young U.S. citizens increasingly use social evaluation tactics to make sense of the information cacophony they experience in digital information environments. The result may be a narrower news diet that consists of congenial information coming from like-minded sources. This scenario comes close to the well-used narrative of filter bubbles. However, in this case, the bubble is being used by young voters as a shield of protection from questionable information and sources. The success of this strategy depends on their initial peer network, the sources young voters have initial trust in, and the permeability of the network. If young voters feel safe in these coherent information networks, they may learn to rely on their smaller circle of sources as a basis for their vote decisions.

Young Voters Turn Away from Current News Sources

Every generation gets politically socialized in a different media environment. The spread of television, the emergence of commercial broadcasting, and the rise of online media were all considered to introduce a "new media" era at their specific times (Bakker and de Vreese 2011; Jennings and Niemi 1968; Mindich 2005; Prior 2007). The ways young citizens experienced media during their formative years are thereby shaping the way these news sources play for the respective generation in the future. Subsequently, citizens will evaluate changes in the media environment in comparison to the media that citizens got to know when they were young. Voters who grow up during the current disinformation debate may view media as something that cannot be trusted and avoid current news sources in the long run.

In the third scenario, youth will grow up and keep a distance from the institution of news media, if they perceive the media as untrustworthy. In five of the eight Western European countries surveyed, younger adults trust the news media less than those in the oldest age group (Matsa et al. 2018). This can be seen as a first indication that "the" news media have a hard time playing a decisive role in informing young voters about political issues. In addition to the danger of young people tuning out from the news because of a lack of interest (Edgerly 2017; Mindich 2005), there is also the possibility of young voters avoiding the news because they feel that they cannot trust it, although recent evidence does not suggest this relationship for the general population (Goyanes, Ardèvol-Abreu, and Gil De Zúñiga 2023). It is unlikely, however, that the distance to the institution of news media will be total and result in news avoidance for a whole generation.

An avoidance of news would not necessarily mean retraction from a public debate or from civic duties, such as turning out in an election. News avoidance during the COVID-19 pandemic, for instance, was found to slightly increase the civic engagement of citizens in activities related to the pandemic (Ohme et al. 2022). If this generation of young voters feels distant to the institution of news media but wants to take part in civic life, the question is what kind of information they will rely on. Alternative news sources that win their trust are one possible option. Receiving information "firsthand" from political actors is another possibility, which often lacks independent verification mechanisms that journalism offers. Finally, given the major role that peer networks play for young voters, it is conceivable that they might rely more strongly on information they receive through (mediated) peer conversations (Cotter and Thorson 2022). In that sense, news media will continue to lose influence in informing this new generation, whereas sources that are acting on particular interests gain in importance and affect political decision-making.

The youngest generation of voters came of age in a time when almost unlimited information was available in the digital space. They grew up with Wikipedia freely available, and smartphones made it and many other sources of knowledge ubiquitous. The youngest cohort of citizens knows how to find, share, and re-create information within seconds. Their vast use of digital platforms like YouTube or Instagram can also be explained by their ability to filter and organize information in an effective manner—something that older Internet users can struggle with quite a bit. In many ways, this youngest generation is more knowledgeable about the digital environment. They vastly outnumber older generations in knowledge about private browsing modes, ownership of WhatsApp and Instagram, and two-factor authentication. This "knowledge gap," however, is narrower for questions of privacy policies, net neutrality, or ad revenue (Vogels and Anderson 2019). Being "digitally smart" does not necessarily translate into greater media literacy, as many scholars have noted (for example, Bennett, Maton and Kervin 2008; Livingstone 2009). However, young voters who feel an advantage in digital literacy compared to older citizens might have higher self-confidence when evaluating media content. Brosius, Ohme, and de Vreese (2021), for example, found that accuracy and impartiality were less important for millennials and Generation Z when evaluating media trust.

As Flanagin and Metzger (2008) have put it, there is a greater uncertainty for young citizens about who is responsible for information and whether it can be believed. The perception of disinformation as a societal problem and the low levels of trust, combined with the feeling of being literate enough to maneuver the digital space, can lead to high levels of news engagement in a different way: Some young voters may become overly obsessed with and hypercritical of the accuracy of information. As a result, they engage more strongly with the intention of the message than with the message itself. Chances are that such a scenario is especially likely in a partisan news context, yet it is cumbersome and requires a certain level of resources. Therefore, it is likely that young voters with higher levels of political interest, efficacy, and knowledge more than ever will engage with political news they come across. However, hyper-critical engagement with news may impede forces that otherwise could have been used to turn news engagement into higher levels of political participation (Andersen et al. 2022). Subsequently, growing up with disinformation can create a generation that knows all about the message but little about the message's content, and this could have detrimental effects on democratic behavior. Young voters with fewer resources and lower digital literacy, in turn, would not show these high levels of news engagement. The "literacy gap" would then not only run between, but also within, generations and increase political information disparities.

Young Voters Turn into Role Models in Navigating Ambiguity

Uncertainty about the source and context of information is the ultimate challenge of growing up in times of surging disinformation. A young generation that is aware of this ambiguity can turn this knowledge into an asset when fighting disinformation. Messages that are produced to deceive are only as effective in influencing opinion formation and voting decisions as there are people who believe them.

As an analogy, the older generation perceived commercials as an accurate type of product description, but younger generations grew up knowing that advertising will tell them almost anything to convince them to buy a product. Still, a large segment of consumers is able to find products that fit their needs, has learned to compare different offers, and can identify phony sales offers. Growing up with the awareness of disinformation helps the transition from a high level of trust in all information with the look and feel of news toward a more critical stance toward information that can be found online. Young citizens can use their digital skills to understand the context of information. They may be quick in running a reverse image search, identifying the owner of a social media account, and having the means to inspect the origin of shared information. If young voters do not know about these strategies so far, a plethora of programs around the world is supporting them in teaching how to spot, and prevent the sharing of, disinformation (for example, Lie Detectors 2019). Of course, the pressing question is, "Will they do that?" As in any generation, only some young voters will use their skills to question the information that they are exposed to. The crucial difference is that the latest generation becomes politically socialized with this legitimate doubt in information and media. Although they may have better things to do than to challenge all information they receive, in critical moments their socialization with disinformation can shield them from being deceived too easily.

If this generation learns more quickly than others how to spot and navigate around disinformation, they can pass on their skills to their older siblings, parents, or even grandparents, and therefore become role models in dealing with disinformation. And if this is too much to ask, they can function as a constant reminder for older generations to deal with digital information more carefully. In this scenario, the skills needed and efforts to be made in finding a routine handling of disinformation will clearly ask more from this new generation than what was required by their parent generations when using news. They will thereby develop strategies to minimize the efforts on receiving reliable information about political developments. If, despite the prevalence of disinformation, Generation Z voters experience that information from journalistic news brands can be trustworthy and even helpful to them, they might be able to save their breath in fighting political disinformation in disparate online spaces and turn back to news sources their parents have trusted. This can result in a comeback of legacy media in a digital space. By being a role model to older generations and turning to trusted sources, young voters may not only be able to form more reliable vote decisions, but also to stop the rise of disinformation in society.

Young Voters and Disinformation—
What We Can Already Say

From the five outlined scenarios, most readers may favor the one in which young voters are socialized in a media environment where disinformation is a known problem and their experience with such disinformation helps them to spot and navigate around deceptive information, leading them to support high-quality journalism and ultimately enabling them to educate others. But how likely are any of these scenarios? While only the future can tell us, it is worth looking for indications in recent research and observations that help us to understand the direction in which this generation is heading.

Low Skills in Detecting Disinformation on Social Media

"Refugees in Germany receive 700 Euro of Christmas bonus." This fake news was circulated mostly in German right-wing circles. It was evaluated as correct by the majority of fourteen- to fifteen-year-old German students in a school lesson where a journalist from the project Lie Detectors visited them (Lie Detectors 2019). Additionally, in an online experiment with over thirty-four hundred sixteen-year-old American high-school students, 52 percent of students perceived a video that provided disinformation about voter fraud to be true. The vast majority of students were at the "beginner" level in a rubric sorting, which means they could not accurately evaluate online content (Breakstone et al. 2019). Minority and disadvantaged students were especially ill prepared to spot deceptive information on social media platforms. With many of these students turning out for the first time in the 2020 U.S. election, there is reason to believe that the first scenario—where young voters rely on disinformation and act on it—is likely to become true, at least in the short term. The youngest cohort of voters mostly receives their political information during an election campaign from social media platforms, where political disinformation spreads most easily (Ohme 2019; Vosoughi, Roy, and Aral 2018). This increases the likelihood that young voters in an upcoming election will get in touch with inaccurate information.

Platforms like Facebook and Twitter have started slowly to contain the spread of mis- and disinformation, with mixed results (Center for Countering Digital Hate 2020). For platforms with greater popularity among young citizens—such as TikTok, Instagram, or WhatsApp—we know little about how they are used to spread disinformation and, therefore, increase the risk of young people coming into contact with it. And we should not forget that this young generation mostly receives news on their smartphones (Kalogeropoulos 2019). The small screens and disturbing usage environments provided by smartphones can make it difficult to differentiate between accurate and false information, as following up on information is cumbersome and details can be overlooked (Dunaway et al. 2018; Ohme et al. 2022; Searles, Feezell, and Rose 2019). Furthermore, the behavior of news snacking is prevalent among young citizens on social media, and most information is only processed on a headline level (Ohme and Mothes 2020). All of this makes it very likely that young voters will be impacted by disinformation in the coming years. It is an open question, however, whether or not they will act on false news sources. Although young voters use social media to inform themselves during election campaigns, there is evidence that media effects are rather small for them when forming a vote decision, whereas other types of campaign engagement—such as visiting an election event or using a vote advice application—are more important (Ohme, de Vreese, and Albæk 2018).

Social Evaluation of News on Private Online Platforms

Young citizens actively curate their social media diets and are therefore able to narrow down their news repertoires, as scenario two suggests. The social filtering on these platforms, and the fact that young people are "cognitive misers" (Fiske and Taylor 1991) who like to minimize the risk of encountering false information, speak to the idea that this new generation narrows down their news repertoires. On the other hand, the possibility of inadvertent news exposure on these platforms and the fact that younger citizens use a higher number of online news sources (Fletcher and Nielsen 2018) does provide counter-evidence for the thesis of shrinking repertoires. Increasingly, however, young people use private online platforms, such as WhatsApp, to share and discuss the news, especially with contacts to whom strong social ties exist (Vermeer et al. 2020). Here, news usage becomes an inherently social process, where exposure and social evaluation occur almost synchronously, as we also found in a study during the COVID-19 outbreak (Ohme et al. 2020). Hence, while the digital infrastructure of social media platforms makes it difficult for young citizens to restrict the sources that they receive news from, they partly retreat into their inner personal circles to process the news (see Cotter and Thorson 2022). On the one hand, close personal ties can shield young voters from disinformation and aid them when forming a vote decision, as they can give guidance and help the voters evaluate information. On the other hand, there is evidence that disinformation spreads quickly, especially in large group chats and on private messaging services. During the 2018 Brazilian presidential election campaign, false information that heavily favored Jair Bolsonaro as one of the presidential candidates was distributed via WhatsApp (Avelar 2019). Hence, online private platforms do not provide a guarantee that people will be shielded from disinformation—rather, the opposite is true. However, the different processes of news engagement on WhatsApp and other platforms can still make a difference. In addition to other positive outcomes, Vermeer and colleagues (2020) found that students' discussion of news on WhatsApp increased their issue-specific knowledge. Narrower news repertoires still put young voters at risk of getting in touch with and being deceived by disinformation, but they may also be one relevant tool for young citizens to learn and become better informed about political issues.

Trusted News Sources Compete for Attention on Social Media

The level to which young people trust the press will determine whether or not they will rely on information disseminated by journalistic news brands for their political decision-making. Looking at the whole information ecology, mis- and disinformation are only spread by a small number of online sources. Most often these are unknown and less trusted sources, and the vast majority of news is still accurate and strives for objective reporting. However, the use of "fake news" as a fighting term amplifies the spill-over from dubious sources to news media in general. Much will depend on whether this strategy of discrediting news media is successful and if the youngest generation will adapt to this understanding. Partly, we see that young citizens trust the news media less than older generations do (Matsa et al. 2018). However, 59 percent of eighteen- to twenty-nine-year-old Americans express high levels of confidence in journalists (Gramlich 2019). Therefore, journalists are one of the few groups that younger citizens have more confidence in than middle-aged and older citizens do. Additionally, although their trust in news media is mediocre, young citizens have far more trust in specific news outlets than older citizens do. Hence, the flagships of journalism are not (yet) sinking when it comes to the credibility that young voters ascribe to them.

The high trust in news sources, however, is in stark contrast to the fact the source of information is less important to young citizens than the platform it is on. Kalogeropoulos (2019) concludes that "news brands play a very small role in young people's lives." There were no news apps among the twenty-five most used smartphone apps of Generation Z members, while Instagram, Facebook, and Snapchat ranked the highest in that data. Most young people are well aware that these platforms can get them in touch with false information, yet they continue to use them frequently (Mitchell et al. 2019). This leaves young voters in a peculiar situation: they consume political information from legacy news sources that they largely trust, but they do so on platforms that are known to spread disinformation. In addition, a great number of other, often more entertaining, content is available on social media. However, posts from political actors and parties compete with a growing amount of microtargeted political advertisement for the attention of young voters (Haenschen and Jennings 2019). Therefore, the usage of social media platforms may be a mixed calculation for young voters, as they risk running into unpleasant and/or deceptive content by making use of the very convenient, personalized, and efficient ways of receiving information on one (or few) platforms. Highly trusted news sources have to fight a hard battle to stay relevant—and, more importantly, visible—in these quickly changing media diets.

So far, there is little indication that being surrounded by disinformation makes young citizens turn their backs on journalistic news sources. Specifically, using the term "fake news" to discredit news organizations seems not to resonate particularly well with them. However, we should remember that increasing numbers of young citizens have started to avoid news in general (Edgerly 2017), and reports suggest that young citizens—and likely older citizens as well—stop getting news from specific outlets or reduce their overall news intake as a response to made-up news (Mitchell et al. 2019). Many studies that look at the youngest cohorts include citizens older than today's first-time voters. Only future studies will show if these differences hold when we look at the first voters among Generation Z.

A Critical Stance toward Online News

Especially in a partisan context, there is a danger that the existence of disinformation turns young citizens hypercritical toward all political information that they receive. This would mean that a generation could habitually engage more with the source and intention of the message than with its actual content. More than twice as many young U.S. citizens agreed that partisan bias is a reason for their lack of trust in news organization (Knight Foundation 2018). In addition, young adults mention revealing details, relying on and citing credible sources, and the completeness of news pieces when they describe what they find trustworthy about news. In the United Kingdom as well as in the United States, the youngest cohort engaged most often in reporting or flagging news posts on social media that they thought were made up (Knight Foundation 2018; Mitchell et al. 2019). Porten-Cheé, Kunst, and Emmer (2020) have recently described the flagging of information as online civic intervention, and thereby a new form of political participation. Evidence exists that it is especially younger male citizens who engage in such actions (Watson, Peng, and Lewis 2019). Additionally, of all of the surveyed reactions to made-up news, young citizens most often mentioned checking the facts of news stories themselves. It is questionable whether they will consistently do so or if it is even reasonable for society to expect this. Yet, it shows there is a growing critical stance to news among this generation, and the majority of them have not given up putting extra effort into the validation of news. In how far this extra engagement with the context and background of the message—rather than with its content—is detrimental to knowledge gains through news exposure is an open question, and therefore it is an important avenue for future research.

High Awareness of Mis- and Disinformation Online

During the recent COVID-19 outbreak, the spread of disinformation online was a highly discussed topic that once again left its marks on the younger generations. A quarter of U.K. citizens aged eighteen to twenty-four said they trusted online news and news on social media now less than before the COVID-19 outbreak (EY Survey 2020). Furthermore, young people are not the only group that has increasingly turned to trusted legacy news sources online (Newman et al. 2020). Although this may be a short-lived effect (Benton 2020), it shows that news still has a high value across all generations, even during, or specifically because of, the ongoing disinformation crisis.

While we see that young citizens react to the disinformation environment they grow up in, they also consider themselves more knowledgeable than older generations about fake news (PWC 2019). But in contrast to the high level of awareness that disinformation is a problem for society, their actual literacy to spot fake news still seems low. Much will depend on how strongly their levels of awareness and literacy converge, and toward which end of the scale. So far, young Americans think that made-up news has a lower impact on the country than older Americans do, and only a minority expects that the problem will get worse (Mitchell et al. 2019). Compared to older cohorts, young citizens blame politicians, activists, journalists, and foreign actors less strongly for the spread of misinformation. Yet, there is one group that young Americans blame most often for the spread of made-up information: the public. It is an open question whether or not pointing their fingers at their own generation means they are already aware that solving the disinformation crisis is ultimately up to them.

If young citizens grow up in a time where it seems necessary to label a news post as false or true, what kind of perception toward the media will they develop? As Van Duyn and Collier (2018) find, it is likely that the discourse about fake news in societal discussions will influence individuals' perceptions of news media. This may have further-reaching consequences for society than the actual damage fake news can do. None of the five potential responses of young voters to disinformation outlined above is likely to become fully true. However, regarding the background of recent patterns of news usage and the attitudes of young citizens, no response seems totally off, either. And while some young voters will not react to disinformation but consume and act on it, others will become resilient and function as role models for older generations.

In the short run, it seems inevitable that, especially through the use of social media as their main gateway to news, young voters will be exposed to disinformation in upcoming election campaigns. The levels of literacy to spot such information are simply too low for us to hope that disinformation simply passes by them. There is little evidence of whether, and how, young voters will act on disinformation. However, if they do, it is likely that their vote decisions will be partly based on inaccurate information.

In the long run, however, the tide may turn. Indications such as a high awareness of disinformation as a problem, high levels of trust in legacy news brands, a frequent engagement in reporting and flagging disinformation, and high skills in curating their own news may help young citizens shielding themselves from disinformation. Realizing these problems and developing such attitudes and skills in their formative years—when the crucial socialization with the political (information) environment takes place—may have long-lasting effects on how this generation deals with disinformation and news in general. The argument that being socialized in an age of disinformation will make young citizens ultimately more resistant to such phenomena seems more valid than only pointing to low levels of literacy.

Learning at a young age to have legitimate doubts about information and to show a healthy skepticism toward online information, that nowadays can just come from anywhere, may be the most effective means to prepare for the spread of disinformation in the future. While the youth have always been better at this than their reputations suggest, it will be difficult for some members of this generation to know when to have doubts and when to trust. The society that expects them to develop informed vote decisions, so that the democratic system can keep running, is also obliged to provide the means and the resources so that a young generation can become more resilient and avoid ever-increasing disparities. If only a share of this new generation learns which news to trust and which to distrust, while another major share falls down the rabbit hole of disinformation, the political system as we know it is likely to be permanently damaged. Therefore, we should provide citizens—especially younger ones who have a harder time figuring out how to navigate this media environment—with the best possible support, good training, high-quality news without paywalls, and effective means to keep disinformation out of the platforms they use. Ultimately, by becoming socialized in a media environment they understand better than older generations do, Generation Z voters will find their own, maybe surprising, ways to respond to misinformation.

REFERENCES

Aalberg, T., and A. T. Jenssen. 2007. "Do Television Debates in Multiparty Systems Affect Viewers? A Quasi-Experimental Study with First-Time Voters." February 19. *Scandinavian Political Studies* 30 (1): 115–35. 10.1111/j.1467-9477.2007.00175.x.

Andersen, K., J. Ohme, C. Bjarnøe, M. J. Bordacconi, E. Albaek, and C. H. De Vreese. 2022. "Generational Gaps in Political Media Use and Civic Engagement." Taylor and Francis. doi.org/10.4324/9781003111498.

Avelar, D. 2019. "WhatsApp Fake News during Brazil Election 'Favoured Bolsonaro.'" October 30. *The Guardian.* www.theguardian.com/world/2019/oct/30/whatsapp -fake-news-brazil-election-favoured-jair-bolsonaro-analysis-suggests.

Bakker, T. P., and C. H. de Vreese. 2011. "Good News for the Future? Young People, Internet Use, and Political Participation." *Communication Research* 38 (4): 451–70. doi.10.1177/0093650210381738.

Bennett, S., K. Maton, and L. Kervin. 2008. "The 'Digital Natives' Debate: A Critical Review of the Evidence." *British Journal of Educational Technology* 39 (5): 775–86. doi.10.1111/j.1467-8535.2007.00793.x.

Bennett, W. L., and S. Livingston. 2018. "The Disinformation Order: Disruptive Communication and the Decline of Democratic Institutions." *European Journal of Communication* 33 (2): 122–39. doi.10.1177/0267323118760317.

Benton, J. 2020. "The Coronavirus Traffic Bump to News Sites Is Pretty Much Over Already." www.niemanlab.org/2020/04/the-coronavirus-traffic-bump-to-news-sites -is-pretty-much-over-already.

Bhatti, Y., and K. M. Hansen. 2012. "The Effect of Generation and Age on Turnout to the European Parliament—How Turnout Will Continue to Decline in the Future." *Electoral Studies* 31 (2): 262–72. doi.10.1016/j.electstud.2011.11.004.

Breakstone, J., M. Smith, S. Wineburg, A. Rapaport, J. Carle, M. Garland, and A. Saavedra. 2019. *Students' Civic Online Reasoning—A National Portrait.* Stanford History Education Group. stacks.stanford.edu/file/gf151tb4868/Civic%20online%20Reasoning %20National%20Portrait.pdf.

Brosius, A., J. Ohme, and C. H. de Vreese. 2021. "Generational Gaps in Media Trust and Its Antecedents in Europe." *International Journal of Press/Politics* 27 (3). doi .org/10.1177/19401612211039440.

Center for Countering Digital Hate. 2020. *#WilltoAct—How Social Media Giants Have Failed to Live Up to Their Claims on the Coronavirus "Infodemic."* 252f2edd-1c8b-49f5 -9bb2-cb57bb47e4ba.filesusr.com/ugd/f4d9b9_17e9f74e84414524bbe9a5b45 afdf77e.pdf.

Cohn, D., and A. Caumont. 2016. "10 Demographic Trends Shaping the U.S. and the World in 2016." March 31. Pew Research Center. www.pewresearch.org/fact-tank /2016/03/31/10-demographic-trends-that-are-shaping-the-u-s-and-the-world/.

Colwell Quarles, R. 1979. "Mass Media Use and Voting Behavior: The Accuracy of Political Perceptions among First-Time and Experienced Voters." October. *Communication Research* 6 (4): 407–36. doi.10.1177/009365027900600402.

Cotter, K., and K. Thorson. 2022. "Judging Value in a Time of Information Cacophony: Young Adults, Social Media, and the Messiness of Do-It-Yourself Expertise." *International Journal of Press/Politics* 27 (3): 629–47. doi.org/10.1177/194016122210 82074.

Doherty, C., J. Kiley, and O. O'Hea. 2018. "Wide Gender Gap, Growing Educational Divide in Voters' Party Identification." March 20. Pew Research Center. www.people -press.org/2018/03/20/wide-gender-gap-growing-educational-divide-in-voters -party-identification/.

Dunaway, J., K. Searles, M. Sui, and N. Paul. 2018. "News Attention in a Mobile Era." March 23. *Journal of Computer-Mediated Communication* 23 (2): 107–24. doi.org /10.1093/jcmc/zmy004.

Edgerly, S. 2017. "Seeking Out and Avoiding the News Media: Young Adults' Proposed Strategies for Obtaining Current Events Information." *Mass Communication and Society* 20 (3): 358–77. doi.org/10.1080/15205436.2016.1262424.

EY Survey. 2020. "Trust in the Media Declines amongst Young People as Fear of Coronavirus Related Fake News Spreads." May 12. EY [Ernst & Young Global Ltd.]. www.ey.com/en_uk/news/2020/05/trust-in-the-media-declines-amongst-young -people-as-fear-of-coronavirus-related-fake-news-spreads-ey-study-finds.

Fiske, S. T., and S. E. Taylor. 1991. *Social Cognition.* McGraw-Hill.

Flanagin, A. J., and M. J. Metzger. 2008. "Digital Media and Youth: Unparalleled Opportunity and Unprecedented Responsibility." In A. J. Flanagin and M. J. Metzger, eds., *Digital Media, Youth, and Credibility,* 5–28. MIT Press.

Fletcher, R., and R. K. Nielsen. 2018. "Are People Incidentally Exposed to News on Social Media? A Comparative Analysis." *New Media and Society* 20 (7): 2450–68. doi.10.1177/1461444817724170.

Goyanes, M., A. Ardèvol-Abreu, and H. Gil De Zúñiga. 2023. "Antecedents of News Avoidance: Competing Effects of Political Interest, News Overload, Trust in News Media, and 'News Finds Me' Perception." *Digital Journalism* 11 (1): 1–18. doi.org/10 .1080/21670811.2021.1990097.

Gramlich, J. 2019. "Young Americans Are Less Trusting of Other People—And Key Institutions—Than Their Elders." August 6. Pew Research Center. www.pewre search.org/fact-tank/2019/08/06/young-americans-are-less-trusting-of-other -people-and-key-institutions-than-their-elders/.

Guess, A., J. Nagler, and J. Tucker. 2019. "Less Than You Think: Prevalence and Predictors of Fake News Dissemination on Facebook." January 9. *Science Advances* 5 (1). doi.10.1126/sciadv.aau4586.

Haenschen, K., and J. Jennings. 2019. "Mobilizing Millennial Voters with Targeted Internet Advertisements: A Field Experiment." January 11. *Political Communication* 36 (3): 1–19. doi.10.1080/10584609.2018.1548530.

Hameleers, M., A. Brosius, F. Marquart, A. C. Goldberg, E. van Elsas, and C. H. de Vreese. 2021. "Mistake or Manipulation? Conceptualizing Perceived Mis- and Disinformation among News Consumers in 10 European Countries." April 5. *Communication Research* 49 (7). doi.org/10.1177/0093650221997719.

Hanitzsch, T., A. van Dalen, and N. Steindl. 2018. "Caught in the Nexus: A Comparative and Longitudinal Analysis of Public Trust in the Press." *International Journal of Press/Politics* 23 (1): 3–23. doi.10.1177/1940161217740695.

Jennings, M. K., and R. Niemi. 1968. "Patterns of Political Learning." *Harvard Educational Review* 38 (3): 443–67. doi.10.17763/haer.38.3.91784021110jw387.

Kalogeropoulos, A. 2019. "How Younger Generations Consume News Differently." *Digital News Report.* www.digitalnewsreport.org/survey/2019/how-younger -generations-consume-news-differently/.

Kim, Y. M., J. Hsu, D. Neiman, C. Kou, L. Bankston, S. Y. Kim, R. Heinrich, R. Baragwanath, and G. Raskutti. 2018. "The Stealth Media? Groups and Targets behind Divisive Issue Campaigns on Facebook." *Political Communication* 35 (4): 515–41. doi .10.1080/10584609.2018.1476425.

Klinger, U., and J. Svensson. 2015. "The Emergence of Network Media Logic in Political Communication: A Theoretical Approach." *New Media and Society* 17 (8): 1241–57. doi.org/10.1177/1461444814522952.

Knight Foundation. 2018. "Indicators of News Media Trust." knightfoundation.org /reports/indicators-of-news-media-trust/.

Lau, R. R., and D. P. Redlawsk. 2001. "Advantages and Disadvantages of Cognitive Heuristics in Political Decision Making." *American Journal of Political Science* 45 (4): 951. doi.10.2307/2669334.

Lie Detectors. 2019. "Tackling Disinformation Face to Face: Journalists' Findings from the Classroom." lie-detectors.org/wp-content/uploads/2019/09/JournalistsFind ings_final.pdf.

Livingstone, S. 2009. "Enabling Media Literacy for 'Digital Natives'—A Contradiction in Terms?" In "Digital Natives": A Myth? POLIS, London School of Economics and Political Science, 4. pdfs.semanticscholar.org/94a5/12330fa1ca8ed5fad4cbe 3619841f03af62.pdf.

Marquart, F., J. Ohme, and J. Möller. 2020. "Following Politicians on Social Media: Effects for Political Information, Peer Communication, and Youth Engagement." *Media and Communication* 8 (2): 12. doi.10.17645/mac.v8i2.2764.

Matsa, K. E., L. Silver, E. Shearer, and M. Walker. 2018. "Western Europeans under 30 View News Media Less Positively, Rely More on Digital Platforms Than Older Adults." October 30. Pew Research Center. www.journalism.org/2018/10/30/despite -overall-doubts-about-the-news-media-younger-europeans-continue-to-trust -specific-outlets/.

Mindich, D. T. Z. 2005. *Tuned Out: Why Americans Under 40 Don't Follow the News.* Oxford University Press.

Mitchell, A., J. Gottfried, G. Stocking, M. Walker, and S. Fedeli. 2019. "Many Americans Say Made-Up News Is a Critical Problem That Needs to Be Fixed." June 5. Pew

Research Center. www.journalism.org/2019/06/05/americans-see-made-up-news
-as-a-bigger-problem-than-other-key-issues-in-the-country/.

Neuberger, C., A. Bartsch, R. Fröhlich, T. Hanitzsch, C. Reinemann, and J. Schindler.
2023. "The Digital Transformation of Knowledge Order: A Model for the Analysis
of the Epistemic Crisis." *Annals of the International Communication Association* 47
(2): 1–22. doi.org/10.1080/23808985.2023.2169950.

Newman, N., R. Fletcher, A. Schulz, S. Andi, and R. K. Nielsen. 2020. *Reuters Institute
Digital News Report 2020*, 112. reutersinstitute.politics.ox.ac.uk/sites/default/files
/2020-06/DNR_2020_FINAL.pdf.

Nicholson, S. P., C. J. Carman, C. M. Coe, A. Feeney, B. Fehér, B. K. Hayes, C. Kam, J. A.
Karp, G. Vaczi, and E. Heit. 2018. "The Nature of Party Categories in Two-Party
and Multiparty Systems: The Nature of Party Categories." *Political Psychology* 39:
279–304. doi.org/10.1111/pops.12486.

Ohme, J. 2019. "When Digital Natives Enter the Electorate: Political Social Media Use
among First-Time Voters and Its Effects on Campaign Participation." *Journal of
Information Technology & Politics* 16 (2): 119–36. doi.org/10.1080/19331681.2019.16
13279.

———. 2023. "News Snacking and Political Learning: Changing Opportunity Structures of Digital Platform News Use and Political Knowledge." March 28. *Journal of Information Technology and Politics*, 1–15. doi.org/10.1080/19331681.2023.21
93579.

———, K. de Bruin, Y. de Haan, S. Kruikemeier, T. G. L. A. van der Meer, and R. Vlie-
genthart. 2022. "Avoiding the News to Participate in Society? The Longitudinal
Relationship between News Avoidance and Civic Engagement." June 25. *Communications* 48(4). doi.org/10.1515/commun-2021-0099.

———, C. H. de Vreese, and E. Albæk. 2018. "The Uncertain First-Time Voter: Effects
of Political Media Exposure on Young Citizens' Formation of Vote Choice in a
Digital Media Environment." *New Media and Society* 20 (9): 3243–65. doi.org/10
.1177/1461444817745017.

———, and C. Mothes. 2020. "What Affects First- and Second-Level Selective Exposure
to Journalistic News? A Social Media Online Experiment." *Journalism Studies* 21
(9): 1220–42. doi.org/10.1080/1461670X.2020.1735490.

———, K. Searles, and C. H. de Vreese. 2022. "Information Processing on Smartphones
in Public Versus Private." October 29. *Journal of Computer-Mediated Communication* 27 (6). doi.org/10.1093/jcmc/zmac022.

———, M. M. P. Vanden Abeele, K. Van Gaeveren, W. Durnez, and L. De Marez. 2020.
"Staying Informed and Bridging 'Social Distance': Smartphone News Use and
Mobile Messaging Behaviors of Flemish Adults during the First Weeks of the

COVID-19 Pandemic." *Socius: Sociological Research for a Dynamic World* 6: 1–14. doi.org/10.1177/2378023120950190.

O'Keefe, G. J., and J. Liu. 1980. "First-Time Voters: Do Media Matter?" *Journal of Communication* 30 (4): 122–29.

Porten-Cheé, P., M. Kunst, and M. Emmer. 2020. "Online Civic Intervention: A New Form of Political Participation Under Conditions of a Disruptive Online Discourse." *International Journal of Communication* 14: 514–34. doi.org/514-534.

Prior, M. 2007. *Post-Broadcast Democracy: How Media Choice Increases Inequality in Political Involvement and Polarizes Elections.* Cambridge University Press.

PWC. 2019. "Fake News Ergebnisse einer Bevölkerungsbefragung [Fake News—Results of a Representative Population Survey]." PWC. docs.dpaq.de/14853-pwc_berichts band_fake_news.pdf.

Schifferes, S., N. Newman, N. Thurman, D. Corney, A. Göker, and C. Martin. 2014. "Identifying and Verifying News through Social Media: Developing a User-Centered Tool for Professional Journalists." *Digital Journalism* 2 (3): 406–18. doi.10 .1080/21670811.2014.892747.

Searles, K., J. Feezell, and P. Rose. 2019. "Attention to Fake News in Mobile Facebook Feeds." Paper presented at ICA 2019, Washington, DC.

Tandoc, E. C. Jr., Z. W. Lim, and R. Ling. 2018. "Defining 'Fake News.'" *Digital Journalism* 6 (2): 137–53. doi.10.1080/21670811.2017.1360143.

Thorson, K. 2020. "Attracting the News: Algorithms, Platforms, and Reframing Incidental Exposure." *Journalism* 21 (8): 1067–82. doi.org/10.1177/1464884920915352.

Van Aelst, P., J. Strömbäck, T. Aalberg, F. Esser, C. de Vreese, J. Matthes, D. Hopmann, S. Salgado, N. Hubé, A. Stępińska, S. Papathanassopoulos, R. Berganza, G. Legnante, C. Reinemann, T. Sheafer, and J. Stanyer. 2017. "Political Communication in a High-Choice Media Environment: A Challenge for Democracy?" *Annals of the International Communication Association* 41 (1): 3–27. doi.10.1080/23808985 .2017.1288551.

Van Duyn, E., and Collier, J. 2018. "Priming and Fake News: The Effects of Elite Discourse on Evaluations of News Media." September 12. *Mass Communication and Society* 22 (1): 29–48. doi.10.1080/15205436.2018.1511807.

Vermeer, S. A. M., S. Kruikemeier, D. Trilling, and C. H. de Vreese. 2020. "WhatsApp with Politics?! Examining the Effects of Interpersonal Political Discussion in Instant Messaging Apps." June 17. *International Journal of Press/Politics* 26 (2). doi.10.1177/1940161220925020.

Vogels, E. A., and M. Anderson. 2019. "Americans and Digital Knowledge in 2019." October 9. Pew Research Center. www.pewresearch.org/internet/2019/10/09 /americans-and-digital-knowledge/.

Vosoughi, S., D. Roy, and S. Aral. 2018. "The Spread of True and False News Online." March 9. *Science* 359 (6380): 1146–51. doi.10.1126/science.aap9559.

Watson, B. R., Z. Peng, and S. C. Lewis. 2019. "Who Will Intervene to Save News Comments? Deviance and Social Control in Communities of News Commenters." *New Media and Society* 21 (8): 1840–58. doi.10.1177/1461444819828328.

Conclusion

• • •

LANCE PORTER

Disinformation around Donald Trump has effectively convinced a large percentage of our electorate in the United States that our election system is fraudulent. While our voting systems seem to have passed several stress tests since 2016, we are facing monumental challenges in our media systems in our upcoming elections. Trump supporters were motivated enough by disinformation to storm the Capitol on January 6, 2021. Some of the same people who claimed in the past that "Blue Lives Matter" beat Capitol police officers with American flags. A mob erected gallows on the Capitol grounds, forced their way through police barricades, crawled through broken Capitol windows, and roamed the halls, chanting "hang Mike Pence." What can be done about disinformation to make sure this does not happen again in our next election?

The contributors to this book gathered for a panel called "The Disinformation Effect: The Manipulation of Political Discourse" as part of the LSU Manship School of Mass Communication's Breaux Symposium in March of 2020, and reckoned with the question of how we can begin to combat disinformation. The interaction among the authors offers some key insights on disinformation—and perhaps even some hope.

Disinformation Is Systemic

There was much talk to the students in the room about how we can train individuals to resist disinformation, particularly young people who are just joining the voting ranks. As the University of Amsterdam's Jakob Ohme put it, "this whole area of disinformation we live in right now hits young people at a special point in time, namely when they develop their political self and also their strategies for how to deal with media." However, our panelists agreed that disinformation is a systemic problem, not an individual one. No amount of media-literacy training is going to mitigate the disinformation problem. George Washington University media and public affairs professor Dave Karpf put it succinctly: "So, the fundamental problem is that Facebook and Google cannot solve this on their own. Citizens, we all together, can't solve this on our own. The solution to disinformation is not, 'Let's all become more miserly information consumers or check every reference.'"

In other words, while media-literacy programs may help some individuals, the disinformation problem is something we need to address at the system level. Media-literacy programs are geared toward providing citizens the tools to access and understand media messages. These educational programs are often focused on building critical thinking skills in the hope that individuals can then better evaluate information based on the source of that information. However, that is a large burden for the average citizen to carry. At the most basic level on social media, how do citizens tell the difference between social media posts that are opinion versus those that are news, or between organic versus paid posts, which can be either news or opinion? Many paid posts in social media are deliberately placed within news feeds to resemble organic content. COVID disinformation forced the platforms' hand in regulating inaccurate or misleading content. However, the platforms have opted to stay out of regulating paid ads related to politics.

University of North Carolina professor Shannon McGregor said she believes the platforms should not be working in that capacity, "but Facebook is not going to take any action on it because it's a paid political ad, and they've decided they're not going to be the arbiters of paid political truth. . . . But I 100 percent do not believe that Facebook or Google or Twitter or Google subsidiary YouTube has the legitimacy or the capacity to make these decisions about what is truth."

Technology Cannot Save Us

Our panelists warned against the technological determinist idea that technology will always change society for the better. Hacker, cybersecurity expert, and Louisiana State University computer science professor Golden Richard III agreed that individuals cannot solve this problem, but that does not mean we cannot rely on technology for help:

> I think we can't simply abandon people to be on their own and try to come up with their own solutions just like we can't do that in cybersecurity. That said, 100 percent bulletproof cybersecurity is impossible. And so, my students and I sob every day as our new technique for solving some cybersecurity issue's blown away, but that doesn't mean you can just quit. The average user's view of the things that are possible in terms of cyberattacks against their computer systems, I think, is largely incomplete because they literally can't imagine how bad the situation is. So, the example I usually use is like someone that locks their office and checks the lock the next day and doesn't see that it's been broken open and the alarm is still on and the windows are not broken, and stuff like that, assumes that stuff that's in their desk is still there and untampered with, and so forth. But from a cybersecurity standpoint, it's literally like people can reach through solid walls, tamper with your stuff and withdraw their hands, and you can't see it. There's malware in all sorts of devices that it's outside the scope of antivirus to scan. So, users are really in a mess.

Disinformation Is an Elite Problem,
Not a Mass Problem

Media-effects research tells us that the effects of any campaign are complicated. Many factors are at play in forming political opinions and making voting decisions. How knowledgeable are individuals? What is their socioeconomic background? How have they voted in the past, and perhaps most importantly, who is within their personal network? According to Karpf, uninformed voters look to elites in making voting decisions, and elites are responsible for much of the disinformation in our political system:

> We have a set of elites now who have come to believe you can just lie and nothing bad will happen. You can release doctored videos, and while the *New York Times* will say, "That's a doctored video," your supporter class will say, "Eh, the *New York Times* is fake news." Or they will just attack the *New York Times* and then keep on going. And what we've learned is, the elite who does that will fundraise a lot of money and not face electoral consequences. That is how we get to a point where our regulatory state stops regulating entirely. It is an elite-level problem, not a mass problem. And that brings me back to the reason why I don't think we can solve this through literacy. Literacy, if we pour all of our time and energy into it, might help our masses be slightly better at identifying disinformation. But it is not going to give us a set of political elites who once again believe in the myth of the attentive public and behave as though, if I am caught lying, bad things will happen. Ergo, I shouldn't lie. So, if we're going to get a government that actually takes governance seriously, we need to start by demanding more of our elites and not instead focusing on us as masses all just being better and then hoping that it trickles up.

Journalists Have a Part to Play

University of Georgia professor Itai Himelboim said, "The problem is not disinformation. The problem is truth doesn't matter." If the platforms are not the arbiters of truth, who is? Journalists are supposed to hold elites accountable. However, a common theme across Kansas State University professor Jacob Groshek's work on journalists and social media is that journalists in the United States are reluctant to enter the fray: "they didn't want to somehow be seen as endorsing messages or responding to groups that were fringe or spreading misinformation, or things like that, because it was a sort of professional hazard." Northeastern University PhD candidate Claudia Flores-Saviaga pointed out that, if journalists do not participate in conversations around contentious issues, extremists and trolls will fill that gap: "It's created an information void, meaning that neutral conversations have not happened anymore and these extreme voices are the ones that are participating more and more."

There is evidence from Flores-Saviaga's and University of Texas professor Josephine Lukito's work that foreign actors used that void to infiltrate social media communities. Lukito has some concrete suggestions for journalists:

> To me, it is still disinformation if the identity is not real. So, for example, a lot of the Russian IRA activity that ended up in news media were actually opinions and not factual pieces of information, and those are a lot harder to verify. And one of the things I've been encouraging newsrooms to do is to try to actually not just take the Tweet and embed it, but to go beyond DMing them, try to call them or email them and make sure that that's a real, verifiable person. Because otherwise, it's quite hard to verify whether an opinion is factually accurate or not. And we do see a lot of Russian trolls pretend to be, for example, Black veterans. They pretend to be LGBTQ or queer folk, and a variety of personae that are American personae that are not real.

Groshek added that journalists could make better use of technology to further engage in these communities to fill this void:

> I think there has to be a value that's assigned to engaging with individuals and actors and accounts on social media. And at the risk of pushing the bot question too far here, there's a lot of instances where we have accounts that are not just bots and not just humans, but humans who will use bits of code to help amplify their messages. So, this may be a way that journalists could start to leverage some technology in a way that is a combination of humans and technology that might make their jobs in some ways a little bit easier.

All in all, the panel agreed that there is no one solution to how much disinformation has infected our media system. It's going to take a combination of systemic solutions related to technology, regulation, and education. We are also going to have to reckon with Trump and the havoc he and his supporters have wreaked on our system long after he has faded from the political scene. This will have to be a bipartisan effort to pursue the truth. In the end, journalists will be key in holding elites accountable to make those changes. The future of U.S. democracy depends on it.

CONTRIBUTORS

Claudia Flores-Saviaga is a PhD candidate in the Citizen AI Lab at Northeastern University. She is also a member of Carnegie's Partnership for Countering Influence Operations research group. Previously she was a fellow at Facebook Research and an intern at Twitter in the Civic Integrity Team. Her research involves the areas of artificial intelligence, crowdsourcing, and social computing. She is interested in understanding how "bad actors" organize disinformation and propaganda messages, and how other citizens organize to debunk those manipulative campaigns. She uses this knowledge to design intelligent systems that can fight disinformation at scale. She started her exploration of online spaces analyzing how political trolls were organizing during the 2016 U.S. presidential elections. Her research has been covered by *Wired,* the Associated Press, *Newsweek,* Buzzfeed, *El País,* and *Slate.*

Jacob Groshek has a long list of research and teaching appointments, including executive director of the Institute for Representation in Sports and Media, the chair of Emerging Media at Kansas State University, as well as an honorary associate professorship at Roskilde University, Denmark. He has been a member of the faculty at Boston University, the Toulouse School of Economics in France, the University of Melbourne in Australia, and Erasmus University in The Netherlands. His areas of expertise address online and mobile media technologies as their uses may relate to sociopolitical and behavioral health change, and include analyses of sports and culture in media content along with user influence in social media.

Itai Himelboim is associate professor of advertising, Thomas C. Dowden Professor of Media Analytics, and the founder and director of the SEE Suite, Social Media Engagement and Evaluation Lab at the University of Georgia. His research interests include social media analytics and network analysis of large social media data, with a focus on the flow of information and misinformation of news in political and international communication. Himelboim studies the network structures that are formed when users interact on social media, including the emergence of network clusters as information echo chambers and the diffusion and sources of content within and across these information silos.

David Karpf is associate professor in the School of Media and Public Affairs at George Washington University. His work focuses on strategic communication practices of political associations in America, with a particular interest in internet-related strategies. Karpf is the award-winning author of *The MoveOn Effect: The Unexpected Transformation of American Political Advocacy* and *Analytic Activism: Digital Listening and the New Political Strategy.* Both books discuss how digital media are transforming the work of political advocacy and activist organizations. His writing about digital media and politics has been published in *Wired, The Nation, Nonprofit Quarterly,* the *Chronicle of Higher Education,* and other publications.

Josephine ("Jo") Lukito is assistant professor at the University of Texas at Austin's School of Journalism and Media and senior faculty research affiliate for the Center for Media Engagement. She studies cross-platform political communication, focusing especially on the hybrid media ecology, disinformation/propaganda, and social media spaces. Lukito specializes in mixed methods and computational approaches to studying language over time. She has published in a variety of journals, including *Political Communication* and *Social Media + Society.*

Jakob Ohme is head of the research group Digital News Dynamics at the Weizenbaum Institute for the Networked Society in Berlin and associated researcher at the Institute for Media and Communication Studies at the Freie Universität Berlin. His research interests center on the impact of digital and mobile communication on news exposure and political behavior with a focus on generational differences in media use and political socialization. He has a special interest in the development of digital methods in political communication and journalism research. Currently, he is a fellow at the Digital Communication Methods Lab at the University of Amsterdam.

Yotam Ophir is assistant professor of communication at the University at Buffalo. His work combines computational methods for text mining, network analysis, experiments, and surveys to study media content and effects in the areas of political, science, and health communication. Ophir is the head of the Media Effects, Misinformation, and Extremism (MEME) Lab, a member of the Center for Information Integrity (CII) at the University at Buffalo, and a distinguished fellow at the Annenberg Public Policy Center at the University of Pennsylvania.

Lance Porter is the Karen W. and Daniel J. King Distinguished Professor in Advertising in the Grady College of Mass Communication at the University of Georgia. Prior to UGA, Porter spent twenty years at Louisiana State University, where he founded the Social Media Analysis and Creation (SMAC) Lab. Porter has focused on digital media since 1995, when he built his first commercial website. As executive director of digital marketing for Disney's film studio and a creative consultant, he has worked on hundreds of film-marketing campaigns. His research focuses on emerging media and brand activism.

Golden G. Richard III is professor of computer science at Louisiana State University and associate director for cybersecurity at the Center for Computation and Technology (CCT) at LSU. He is also a fellow of the

American Academy of Forensic Sciences. Richard has more than forty years of practical experience in computer systems and computer security, and his research interests lie in memory forensics, digital forensics, malware analysis, exploit development, reverse engineering, systems programming, and operating systems.

Saiph Savage is assistant professor and director of the Civic A.l. Lab at the Khoury College of Computer Sciences at Northeastern University. Her research focuses on creating intelligent civic technology to organize collective action for change, which includes battling misinformation and empowering gig and rural workers to access better jobs. Before joining Northeastern in 2021, Savage was a tech worker at Intel Labs and Microsoft Bing, and a crowd research worker at Stanford University. She has taught or directed at West Virginia University, Carnegie Mellon University, and the University of Washington, with an emphasis on human-computer interaction and human-centered design.

Sander Andreas Schwartz is assistant professor of communication studies at Roskilde University. He has done research on and published in peer-reviewed journals mainly within the field of political communication and social media. He is also currently working with projects in relation to datafication, data literacy, and privacy issues online. Schwartz is a cofounder of the Digital Media Lab at Roskilde University, where he is developing digital methods to analyze online communication content and networks. His main interest lies in the critical examination and analysis of digital data, and how this data can be used to benefit a democratic process of political communication.

Dror Walter is assistant professor of digital communication at the Department of Communication at Georgia State University. His research is centered on the intersection between traditional media-effects theories and novel computational social science methods such as machine learning, natural language processing, and network analysis. Specifically, his current research projects focus on two interrelated contexts: extremist forms of political discussion (especially political misinformation) and health misinformation, and the ways in which the two interact in online spaces.

INDEX

accountability, 35
accuracy of information, 15–16, 142, 146
action, facilitating participation, 81
action verbs, 73
active measures, 15–16, 21
active users, 78–80
activists, 68, 73–74
ad revenue, 142
Adult Friend Finder, 94
affordance effects, 129
African American community, 68
AIDS Information Introductory Diskette, 89–90
algorithms, 104, 119, 121–22
Ali-Gombe, Aisha, 104
alternative news sources, 136, 141
Alternative Party (Denmark), 126
alt-right subreddits, 71
AMAs. See Ask Me Anything sessions (AMAs)
anomalous artifacts, 104
anonymity, 12, 19
antisocial behavior, 69
antitrust enforcement, 37, 39
antitrust regulation, 36
antivirus scans, 96–98, 99
application programming interface (STREAM API), 119
Arab Spring movements, 68
artificially gaining followers, 19

Ask Me Anything sessions (AMAs), 77–79
"assembly-line" style of disinformation production, 18
astroturfing, 14, 19
audience metrics, 10, 12–13, 18, 19
authority indicators, 46
automation, 10, 12–13, 18–19, 104–5, 128–29
avoidance of news, 141

backbone extraction, 52–53
backdoors, 88
bad actors, 66–71
"bag of words" approach, 50
Bayesian generative approach, 50
belief echoes, 43
Bennett, Lance, 135
betweenness centrality, 122–27
Biden, Joe, 2, 38
Big Lie of 2020, 1–4
binomial logit link models, 52
birther movement, 3–4
Black activists, 21
Black Lives Matter movement, 68
black propaganda, 10, 11, 12, 15, 23
blockchain technologies, 94
blogs, 16–17
Bolsonaro, Jair, 147
Bonferroni, 51, 54
border wall, U.S., 78

Borra, Erik, 120
botnets, 91–93
bots, 13, 19, 21–22, 75, 81, 86–87, 122,
    123–25, 127–28, 129
bottom-up norms, 25
boycotts, 71
Bradshaw, S., 70
Brandwatch, 49–50
Brazilian presidential election campaign
    of 2018, 147
Breaux Symposium, LSU, 159–64
Breitbart News Network, 49, 60
Brenner, S. W., 99
Brexit debate, 114
Brosius, A., 142
bullshit, defined as type of
    disinformation, 10
Bush, administration, 36, 38
Buttry, Steve, 2–3
Bystrov, Mikhail Ivanovich, 17

call to action, 72–75
Cambridge Analytica (CA), 33, 35, 39
campaign engagement, 145–46
candidates of color, 117
Carrier, B., 99
Case, Andrew, 104
CFPB. See Consumer Financial Protection
    Board (CFPB)
chemical warfare, 15
Cheng, J., 69
China, 16, 25
Chinese government, 69–70
CIA, 80
CISA. See Cybersecurity and
    Infrastructure Security Agency (CISA)
citizen activists, 123
citizen journalism, 129
citizens, 123–24, 125, 129
civic engagement, 141
civic technology research, 80
Clinton, Hillary, 71–72, 74
Clinton administration, 38
clustered topic network, 51–54

clustering method, 73
code-pointer integrity, 88–89
cognitive misers, 138, 146
Cold War, 11
collaboration among journalists, 2
collective action, 67–69
collective identity, 80–82
Collier, J., 151
command-and-control servers, 91–92
commercial broadcasting, 140
commercials, 143
communication systems, 25
community detection, 48, 50, 122
computational propaganda, 10, 67
computers, 96–105
confidence in journalists, 148
Congress, U.S., 39
conservative bot accounts, 123–25, 127–28
conservative issues, 53–56
conservatives, 8, 21, 35, 47
conspiracy theories, 34–35, 67, 74, 80, 87
consumer data privacy, 37
Consumer Financial Protection Board
    (CFPB), 37–38
content combining text with images and
    videos, 46
Content Introducers, 47–48, 51–61
Content Spreaders, 47–48, 51–60
control flow, 88–89
correction and change, 43
Cotter, K., 140
COVID-19 pandemic, 93, 95, 117, 141, 147,
    150, 160
Crimea, 18
Crimson Hexagon, 49–50
critical stance toward online news,
    149–50
Cruz, Ted, 2
cryptocurrency, 90
CryptoShuffler, 90
Culotta, A., 68–69
The Curse of Bigness (Wu), 36
cyberattacks, 13, 87, 100–101
cyber-disruption, 69–70

cyber-espionage, 10
cyber-hygiene, 99–100
cyber propaganda, 11
cybersecurity, 86–105
Cybersecurity and Infrastructure Security
    Agency (CISA), 93
cyberwarfare, 10–11, 14
cyber world view, 100

Danish national elections, 114–29;
    election campaign of 2019, 117–19;
    general elections of 2019, 115, 121–23;
    national election of 2015, 134; national
    election of 2019, 125–28
Dansk Folkeparti (Danish People's Party),
    118
darknet operators, 86
data breaches, 94–95
data carving, 101–2
data collection: for the 2018 U.S. midterm
    elections, 120–21; for the 2019 Danish
    general elections, 121–23
data-driven approach, 48–49
Data Execution Prevention (DEP), 88, 89
data voids, 67, 79–80, 82
DDOS. *See* denial-of-service attacks
    (DDOS)
debunking disinformation, 79–80, 82
deception, 11, 133
deep fakes, 86
defensive cybersecurity, 89
democracy, 42–43, 164
democratic institutions, 11, 23–24, 25,
    86–87
Democrats, 9, 117
denial-of-service attacks (DDOS), 95
Denmark, 6, 115, 119, 126, 127–28, 129
DEP (Data Execution Prevention), 88
Descartes, 100
descriptive data, 50
deviant groups, 69–70
de Vreese, C. H., 142
digital affordances, 12, 19
digital blackfacing, 21

digital communication, 10, 12–13, 16, 24
digital data access, 120
digital disinformation, 8–25
digital forensics, 97, 99, 101–3, 105
digital investigative techniques, 96–99
digitalization, 136
digital literacy, 142–43
digitally networked media, 135–36
digital media, 12, 16–17, 37, 136
Digital Methods Initiative—Twitter
    Collection and Analysis Toolkit (DMI-
    TCAT), 119–20, 121, 128
digital natives. *See* young voters
digital platforms, 10, 32–40
digital political communication, 33, 35
digital skills, 143–44
digital voter-suppression efforts, 35
"Directorate D" department, 15
DiscoverText, 120
disinformation, 3–4; avoidance of news,
    141; botnets, 91–93; bots, 127–28;
    campaigns around the world, 24–25;
    as a cybersecurity problem, 86–87;
    debunking, 79–80, 82; defined, 9;
    digital literacy, 142–43; disinformation
    order, 135–37, 138; elite problem,
    not a mass problem, 162; fake news,
    135–37; five responses of young voters
    to, 137–38; growing up with, 133–35,
    138, 143; high awareness of, 150–51;
    incentivization of malware, 89–91; is
    systemic, 160–61; journalists, 163–64;
    Latinx social media, 66–83; online
    news, 149–50; Russian disinformation,
    14–24; social evaluation of news on
    private online platforms, 146–47;
    social media platforms, 145–46; social
    media regulation, 36; state-sponsored
    disinformation, 9–25, 114–29; technical
    solutions to combat malware and,
    101–5; Trojan defense, 96–99; trusted
    news sources compete for attention on
    social media, 147–49; uncertain young
    voters in an age of disinformation,

framing, 68–69
fraud, 1–4, 93–94
Fraunhofer Institute for Communication (FKIE), 91
Frederiksen, Mette, 115
Freelon, D., 21
FTC. *See* Federal Trade Commission (FTC)

gamification, 67, 75
Gannett news service, 3
GANs. *See* generative adversarial networks (GANS)
Gaslight platform, 104–5
gatekeeping, 44, 122, 128–29, 138
General Data Protection Regulation (GDPR), 37
generational gaps, 133
Generation Z voters, 132–52
generative adversarial networks (GANs), 86
Gephi application, 119, 121
Gibbs sampling, 50
Giuliani, Rudy, 1
Google, 3, 33–34, 37–39
Google News Lab, 2
government-directed censorship, 36
Graham, Lindsey, 124
grassroots conservatism, 53–55
grassroots networks, 23–24
Groshek, Jacob, 114–29, 122, 163–64
group chats, 147
growing up with disinformation, 133–35, 138, 143. *See also* media literacy
Guardian, 114

hacking, 10, 13
hashtags, 47, 54, 56, 59, 69, 71, 72, 74
hate speech and harassment, 36
heap-exploitation prevention techniques, 89
Hemphill, L., 68–69
Henninger, J., 99
Heston, M., 69

hierarchies in digital communication, 24
high awareness of mis- and disinformation online, 150–51
Himelboim, Itai, 42–61, 47, 163
"Historian" style, 74, 80–81
HIV/AIDS, 15
Homestead Temporary Shelter for Unaccompanied Children, 78
homophily, 46, 47
HookTracer, 105
horizontal and participatory debate, 124–25
House of Representatives, U.S., 116–17
Howard, P., 70
Hugin, Bob, 124
Hurdle count, 57–58
hypercritical engagement of young voters, 142–43
hyperlinks, 46, 48
hyper-partisanship, 24

I2P, 90
illegal immigrants, 78
imaginary demon, Descartes's, 100
immigration, 77, 78
impersonation, 16, 21
inaccuracies in mainstream media reporting, 43–44
inadvertent exposure, 135, 146
incentivization of malware, 89–91
increase of choice in news sources, 137
independents, 134
infected attachments, 92
influential users, 122–29
information monopolies, 37–38
information proliferation, 135–36
information void, 163–64
information warfare, 70
informed vote decisions, 152
in-person voting, 93
Instagram, 142, 145–46, 148
Institute for Representation in Society and Media, 120
internal maintenance of bots, 19

Russia, 8–25, 70
Russian digital disinformation, 16–17
Russian disinformation, 14–25
Russian fake accounts, 46–47
Russian Internet Research Agency. *See*
Internet Research Agency, Russian
(IRA)

SAF. *See* Something Awful Forums (SAF)
sanctuary cities, 77
Sanders, Bernie, 21
satirical hashtags, 71
Savage, S., 66–83
Schwartz, Sander Andreas, 114–29
self-description, 48–49, 52–53, 55–56, 59,
61
self-replicating computer software, 87–88
Senate, U.S., 77, 116–17
shareability, 49, 59, 61
signed kernel drivers, 89
slang, 73, 75, 76, 81
SMAC Lab. *See* Social Media Analysis and
Creation (SMAC) Lab
smartphones, 142, 146, 148
Snapchat, 148
social bots, 87
social currency, 44
Social Democratic Party (Denmark), 126
social engineering, 91
social evaluation of news on private
online platforms, 146–47
social features, 46
social filtering, 140, 146–47
Social-Liberal Party (Denmark), 126
social media, 1–3, 42–61, 115–16; analysis
results, 128–29; botnets, 91–93; and
Danish election campaign of 2019, 118;
data collection, 119–21; disinformation
and Latinx social media, 66–83;
disinformation campaigns across
the world, 24–25; flagging of
information, 149; high awareness
of mis- and disinformation online,
150; Internet Research Agency (IRA),

17–22; journalists, 163–64; learned
information routines, 138; low skills in
detecting disinformation on, 145–46;
and media literacy, 160; narrower
circle of news sources, 139–40; online
diffusion of misinformation, 43–45;
Reddit, 70–83; regulation, 35–36; and
Russian disinformation, 17; social
evaluation of news on private online
platforms, 146–47; state-sponsored
disinformation on social media, 10,
12–14; trusted news sources compete
for attention on, 147–49; and U.S.
midterm elections of 2018, 124–25
Social Media Analysis and Creation
(SMAC) Lab, 2–3
Social Media Research Foundation, 120
social networks, 140
sock puppets, 14, 69
SODDI ("some other dude did it")
defense, 96–99, 102
software bots, 86–87
Something Awful Forums (SAF), 69
spam, 91–92
specialists, 17–18, 20
stack canaries, 88–89
State Department, U.S., 38
state governments, 11, 12, 16
state-sponsored disinformation, 9–25
Steel, C. M., 97
Stewart, L. G., 47
Stone, Roger, 2
StoptheSteal.org, 2
storage devices, 101–3
storming of the U.S. Capitol (January 6,
2021), 2–3, 159
Stram Kurs (Hard Line Party, Denmark),
115, 118, 125–26
STREAM API (application programming
interface), 119
Suarez-Tangil, G., 90
subreddits, 70–71, 74, 76–79
subversive behavior, 75–80, 81
surfing activities, 102–3

surveillance, 12–14, 16, 20, 24
Sweden, 118
system configuration data, analysis of,
     101–2

Tandoc, E. C., Jr., 122
tariffs, 117
techlash, 35–36
technical solutions to combat malware
     and disinformation, 101–5
technology, reliance on, 161
tech platforms, 33–34, 35–36, 39
television, 140
@TEN_GOP, 8–9
Texas, 77
thematic personae, 45–61
Thorson, E., 43
Thorson, K., 140
TikTok, 145–46
timelining, 101–2
top-down norms, 25
topic modeling, 48–50
Tor, 90
translation project, 17
translator project, 20
Trojans, 88, 91–92, 96–99
"The Trojan Horse Defense in
     Cybercrime Cases" (Brenner, Carrier,
     and Henn), 96–97
troll armies, 14, 17, 25
troll farms, 14, 17
trolling behavior, 69–70
"Troll Slang" style, 73, 74, 81
Trump, Donald, 1–4, 8, 21, 22, 33, 35, 38,
     53, 70–72, 74, 78, 114–15, 116–17, 129,
     159, 164
trust, 132–33, 135–37, 139–40, 141, 147–49,
     152
Twitter, 1–2, 8, 10, 19–21, 39–40, 44,
     45–61, 68, 69, 72, 115–16, 118, 123–24,
     125–26, 128–29, 145
Twitter API, 119–20
Twitter bios, 50, 51, 60
Twitter data, 120–21

two-factor authentication, 142
typography of the network, 45

Ukraine, 18, 114
undocumented immigrants, 78
uninformed voters, 162
United Kingdom, 19, 149
United Nations resolution, 25
United States, 9, 11, 19–20, 24, 119, 134,
     149, 163
Univision, 2
unsupervised analysis, 46, 50
USA Really, 19
USA Today, 2
U.S. Census, 77
U.S. Cybersecurity and Infrastructure
     Security Agency report, 100
"useful idiots," 115–16, 125
Usenet participants, 46
userland malware, 105
user-level malware, 88
user networks, 127
users, 45–61, 69, 71, 99–101, 119–29
U.S. national elections, 114–29; election
     of 2016, 1–4, 9, 20–24, 46–47, 66–83,
     116–17, 136; elections of 2020, 1–4,
     38–39, 115, 117, 145; and information
     monopolies, 38–40; midterm elections
     of 2018, 67, 75–80, 81–82, 115, 116–17,
     120–21, 123–25, 126–27; online voting,
     93–95, 100; presidential campaigns of
     2008, 66

vaccine misinformation, 44
Van Duyn, E., 151
verification symbol, Twitter, 46
Vermeer, S. A. M., 146–47
Vietnam War, 15
Vining, Robyn, 124
virality, 42–61
"Viral News" style, 73–74, 81
virtual private networks (VPNs), 13
viruses, 87–88
volatile storage (RAM), 103

voter-suppression efforts, 35
voting behavior, 22, 162
voting periods, 11
voting systems, 93–95, 159

Walter, D., 42–61, 45, 47, 51, 60–61
war dial, 91
wartime, 11
Wasserman Schultz, Debbie, 78
web brigades, 17
web-browser history and caches, 102
wedge issues, 14, 15, 21
Westphalian sovereignty, 11, 24–25
WhatsApp, 10, 142, 145–47
white propaganda, 10, 16, 23
Wikipedia, 95, 142
Windows registry, 101–2
Windows Subsystem for Linux (WSL), 105
within-system changes, 135
women candidates, 117
worms, 88
WSL. *See* Windows Subsystem for Linux (WSL)
Wu, Tim, 36

Xia, Y., 21

Yahoo, 94–95
Yandex, 17
young voters, 132–52; and changes in media environment, 140–41; five responses of, to disinformation, 137–38; growing up with disinformation, 133–35, 138, 143; high awareness of mis- and disinformation online, 150–51; hypercritical engagement with news, 142–43; low skills in detecting disinformation on social media, 145–46; narrower circle of news sources, 139–40; and online news, 149–50; relying and acting on disinformation, 138–39; as role models in dealing with disinformation, 143–44; and social evaluation of news on private online platforms, 146–47; trusted news sources compete for attention of, on social media, 147–49; uncertainty in an age of disinformation, 134–37; where generation is heading, 144–45
YouTube, 142

zero-inflated models, 52, 57–58
Zhang, Y., 23
Zuckerberg, Mark, 32, 36

www.ingramcontent.com/pod-product-compliance
Lightning Source LLC
Chambersburg PA
CBHW030332270326
41926CB00010B/1598